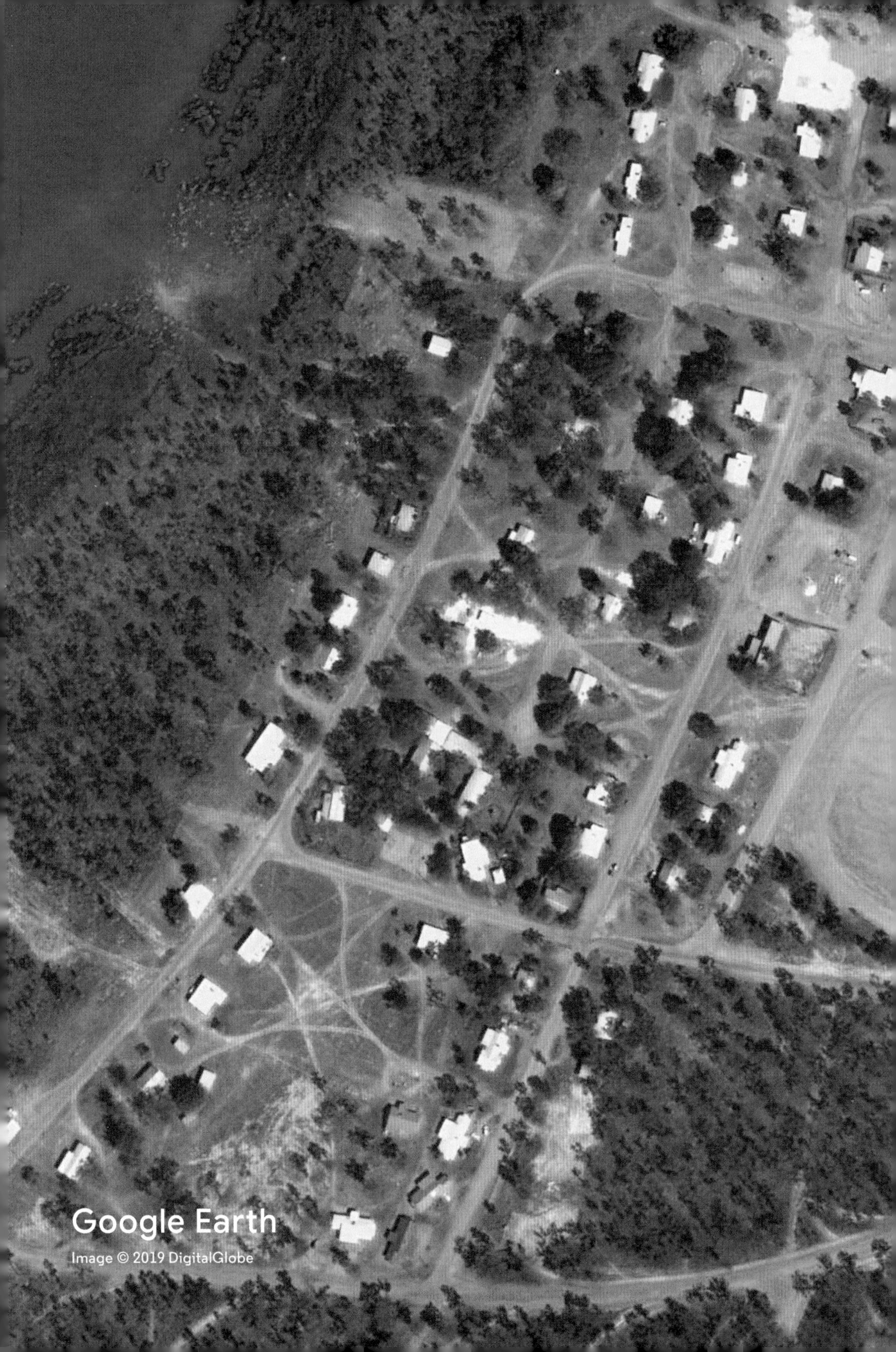
Google Earth
Image © 2019 DigitalGlobe

PHONE & SPEAR A YUTA ANTHROPOLOGY

PHONE & SPEAR A YUTA ANTHROPOLOGY

PHONE & SPEAR
A YUṮA ANTHROPOLOGY

MIYARRKA MEDIA

PAUL GURRUMURUWUY

JENNIFER DEGER

ENID GURUṈULMIWUY

WARREN BALPATJI

MEREDITH BALANYDJARRK

JAMES GANAMBARR

KAYLEEN DJINGADJINGAWUY

 Goldsmiths
Press

Copyright © 2019 Goldsmiths Press
First published in 2019 by Goldsmiths Press
Goldsmiths, University of London, New Cross
London SE14 6NW

Printed and bound by Versa Press, USA

Distribution by the MIT Press
Cambridge, Massachusetts, USA
and London, England

Copyright © 2019 Miyarrka Media

A CIP record for this book is available
from the British Library.

ISBN 978-1-912685-18-9 (pbk)

www.gold.ac.uk/goldsmiths-press

for

FIONA YANGATHU

CONTENTS

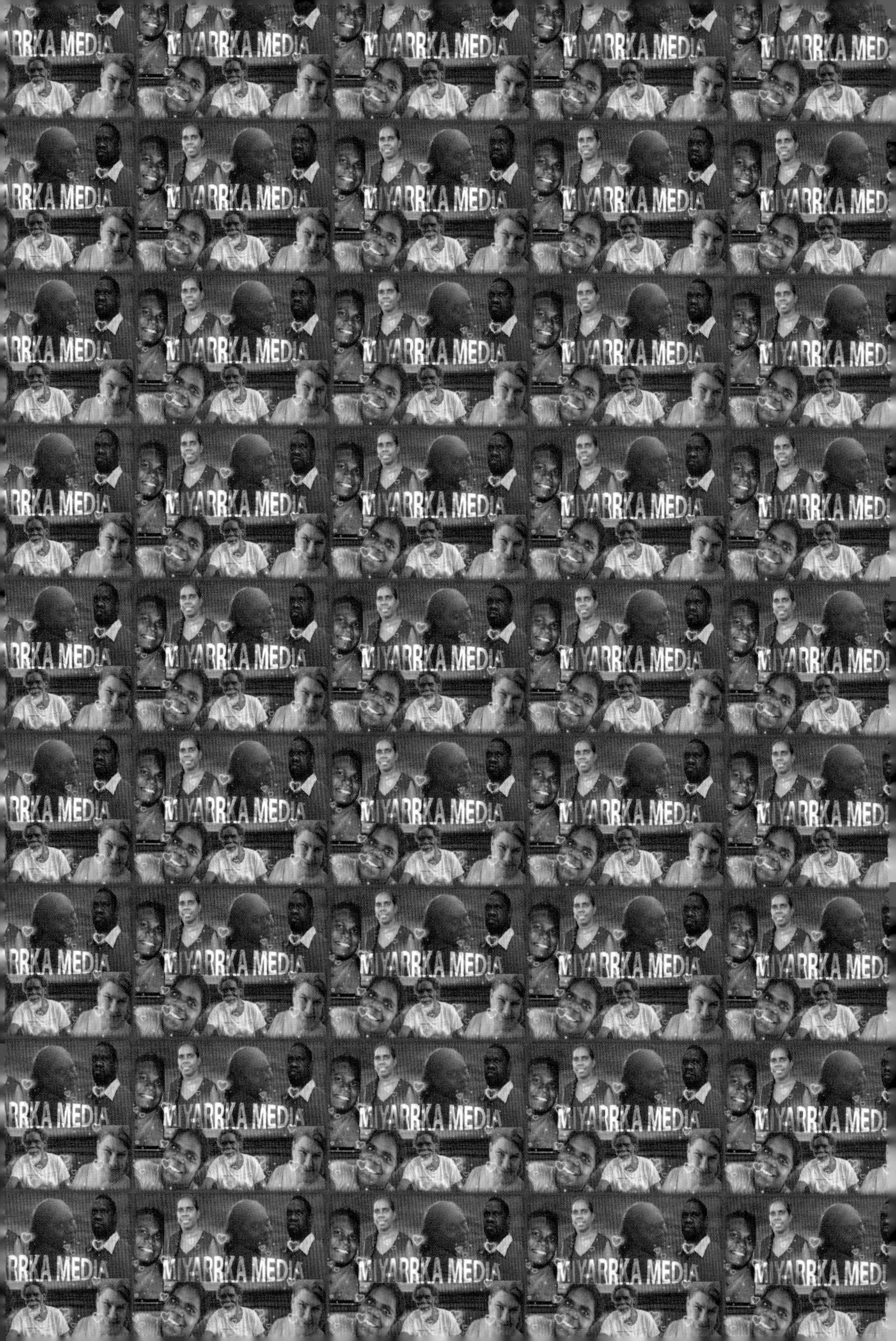
MIYARRKA MEDIA

MIYARRKA MEDIA: WHO WE ARE

PAUL GURRUMURUWUY

Red is my colour, the colour of the Dhaḻwaŋu flag. Through red I can show my clan identity and my connections to my father and his father and his father and his father... going way, way back.

JENNIFER DEGER

Pink was the favourite colour of my Yolŋu ŋändi, Fiona Yangathu. I choose this colour to show my relationship to her, my mother through Yolŋu *gurruṯu* [kinship]. Yolŋu sometimes use the word *biŋk* to refer to non-Aboriginal women, so that's another way to see it.

ENID GURUŊULMIWUY

Green is my *märi* colour, the colour of the Wangurri flag, the colour of my mother's mother's mob.

MIYARRKA MEDIA (previous page)
Simeon Rigamawuy Wunuŋmurra, Jennifer Deger, 2019

WARREN BALPATJI

Purple is what you get when you mix together all the colours of *djäri*, the rainbow of the Gurruwiwi clan.

MEREDITH BALANYDJARRK

Blue is the colour of my *yapa wäŋa*, my sister country, a place called Yalakun. That's where I grew up.

JAMES GANAMBARR

Yellow is my *ŋän̲di* colour, my mother's colour, the yellow of the Gumatj flag.

KAYLEEN DJINGADJINGAWUY

Brown is for me. It is the colour of *guku* [bush honey], the colour of the *gad̲ayka'* stringy bark tree.

BUKU-MANAPANMIRR [JOINING TOGETHER]

JD   *Phone & Spear* is an invitation to participate in a Yolŋu art of connection.

Buku-manapanmirr means joining together. When Yolŋu use this term they point to the potential for people to come together without denying the differences that define us. *Phone & Spear* is an experiment with giving form to this generous Yolŋu capacity for creating mutuality and inclusion, while still allowing for distinctive, and sometimes divergent, points of view. In the design we overtly acknowledge that each member of Miyarrka Media makes sense of the world from our own perspective, according to age, experience and background. Seven voices, assembled side-by-side, marked by different colours, combine here to form a commentary that deliberately refracts our various points of view, allowing us to speak individually—and together. While this style and structure may appear confusing at first, we hope that as you turn the pages you will become attuned to not only to the individual voices, but to the rhythms, patterns and orientations that hold them together.

Language provides another way to demonstrate the generative social potential of joining things together. As my Yolŋu colleagues made clear from the start, this is a work of anthropology, and as such is primarily directed at *balanda*. They therefore saw no reason to produce a fully bilingual text. Nonetheless, we use many Yolŋu terms within the text, sometimes without translation. In doing so we follow Yolŋu linguistic conventions. When Yolŋu speak with non-Aboriginal people in English, they often include Yolŋu terms, adjusting the level of complexity according to how much the person already understands of their language and life. I have found this code-switching convention an extremely effective way to learn and so we decided to adopt it here when transcribing and translating the recorded discussions from which the book has been crafted. The glossary will help if you get lost.

PG   Have a look at the cycad palm standing beside our group *bitja* a couple of pages back. That's my *märi*, it belongs to the land, stories and songs of my mother's mother clan, the Wangurri people. *Märi* is the boss for ceremony and everything, really. *Märi* is our backbone. That's how it is for us. That's *gurruṯu*, what you call family or kinship.

We dedicated the book to my beloved wife who passed away a few years back, Fiona Yangathu. She called that cycad *ŋändi* because she had a Wangurri mother. Putting that photo and her name side-by-side here shows another relationship that is important for Yolŋu, one we call *yothu-yindi* [child-mother]. What I'm telling you is that Yolŋu life is complicated. It has deep patterns and meanings. It has many layers, many riches and responsibilities. You have to know how to look at things, to see those connections and feel them too. That's why we worked hard to make this book, so that you can see, you can feel and you can know.

Together with us. *Buku-manapanmirr.*

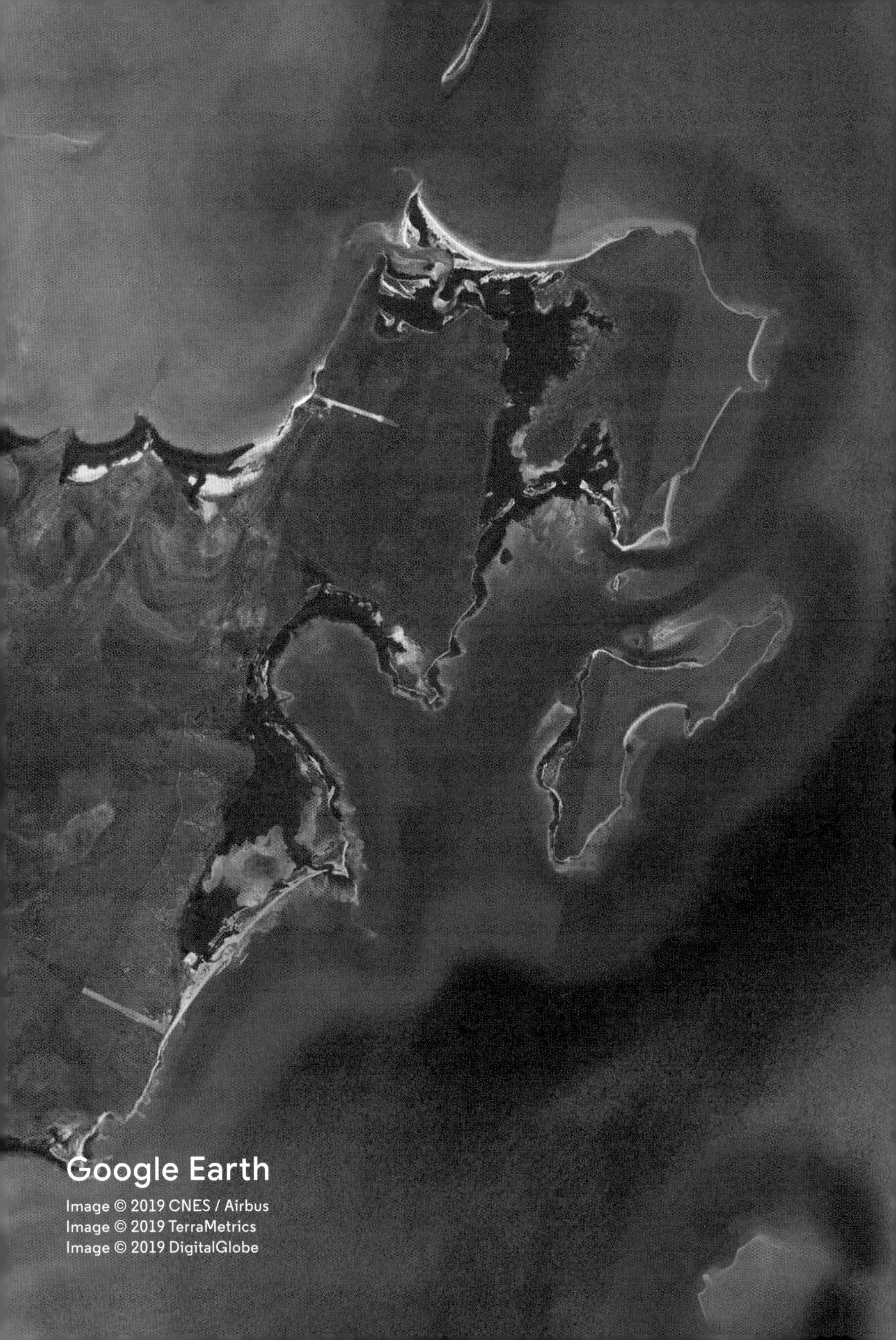

Google Earth

Image © 2019 CNES / Airbus
Image © 2019 TerraMetrics
Image © 2019 DigitalGlobe

What you see now is *wäŋa*. *Wäŋa* means land and home. Or you can say 'country' in English, too. All Yolŋu are related to each other through the *wäŋa* and the *wäŋa* themselves are related to each other. We are related through the sea too. Yolŋu connections do not stop at the beach.

The two airstrips on the left belong to Yalakun (top) and Raymaŋgirr (below). They are just two of the Yolŋu homelands in the Miyarrka region of the Northern Territory. Those two *wäŋa* call each other *yothu-yindi*. Miyarrka Media have close relationships to, and responsibilities for, these particular *wäŋa*, relationships that spread out to other *wäŋa* and other families and tribes, right across Arnhem Land, to Darwin and Cairns and even farther away.

Orthography and Pronunciation Guide

The Yolŋu words in this book are from Dhay'yi (Dhaḻwaŋu) and Dhuwal (Djambarrpuyŋu) languages. The following guide to orthography and pronunciation is adapted from multiple sources.

ä   A long 'a', like in the English word 'star'.

ḏ   Pronounce an English 'd' sound while curling the tongue back so the underside of the tip just touches the roof of the mouth behind the teeth.

dh   Sounds almost like an English 'd', but pronounced with the tip of the tongue poking out between the teeth.

dj   Sounds similar to the English 'j', as in 'jug'. The tongue is pushed forward so that the tip of the tongue is down behind the bottom teeth.

ḻ   Pronounced with tongue curled back. See ḏ.

ṉ   Pronounced with tongue curled back. See ḏ.

nh   An 'n' sound made with the tongue between the teeth.

ny   Similar to the English 'n' in the word 'new'. The tongue is in the same position as for dj.

ŋ   The sound of the 'ng' in the the word 'sing'. It is made with the back of the tongue against the roof of the mouth in the velar position. If you don't have the special character to represent this letter, then you can simply write 'ng'.

o̱   Pronounced with tongue curled back. See ḏ.

ṯ   Pronounced with tongue curled back. See ḏ.

th   Like a hard 't' but with the tongue protruding between the teeth.

rr   A short flapped or rolled 'r' sound.

'   Glottal stop, bringing the word to a quick finish by choking off the air to the syllable.

Image Permissions

The collaged family photographs we share in this book raise issues of rights and responsibilities that extend beyond the specific, and mostly young, artists who created them. Wherever possible, Miyarrka Media sought permission to publish from senior family members, as well as the people who appear in the images. Paul Gurrumuruwuy led what became a lengthy process of consultation and permission-gathering, working image by image, family by family. On several occasions, when a phone call proved inadequate, Gurrumuruwuy flew to other communities to hold formal meetings with family groups.

Special care has been taken with images that feature deceased people. But, as will become clear later in these pages, the fact that an image includes someone who has died does not necessarily restrict its reproduction—provided permission has been sought. Any image deemed unsuitable for public circulation, for whatever reason, has been removed from the manuscript. Generally, however, we have found strong support for publishing these *bitja* [images] as a visual resource for future generations.

The Use of Names in This Book

The members of Miyarrka Media go by many names. Each of us have names that link to ancestral places and stories. We have nicknames and *balanda* [non-Aboriginal] names too. What people call us depends on where we are and who we are talking with. Often, we use *gurruṯu* [kinship] terms. So that person you call *ŋäṉdi* [mother] calls you *waku* [son/daughter] in return. The person you call *märi* [mother's mother or mother's mother's brother] reciprocates by calling you *gutharra* [grandchild through the maternal line].

In the *balanda* world everyone needs a surname. It helps to organise paperwork in the clinic, the school, the tax office and social security databases. Yolŋu have adopted surnames that follow the father's line. These highlight the connection to the groupings that anthropologists call clans, but Yolŋu mostly call tribes when speaking English, taking the term from the Bible. In this book these clan and tribe is used interchangeably. We are not interested in getting bogged down in those kinds of anthropological debates.

But names and naming practices do matter. A lot. We discussed them a lot while making the book and came up with agreed upon conventions following Gurrumuruwuy's example. For although Paul Gurrumuwuy's birth certificate lists his last name as Wungungmurra (a name that shows that he belongs to a specific lineage of the Dhaḻwaŋu clan) he prefers not to use it when he feels it is not necessary. So throughout in his career as a filmmaker, artist, actor and now as a *yuṯa* anthropologist, Gurrmumuruwuy has been asked to be credited without his *balanda* surname. When communicating with *balanda* he chooses to stick with Paul because it's easy for them to remember and pronounce, and Gurru-muruwuy because this name, given to him by his *märi*, linking him directly to his ancestral homeland of Gurrumuru, expresses his Yolŋu identity in a strong and publicly suitable way.

All the members of Miyarrka Media follow this convention here, with the exception of James Ganambarr and Jennifer Deger.

For the photo media artists and the people within the *bitja*, we decided to list surnames in order to create a more comprehensive record for the future.

Finally, we want to let you know that if you are having trouble typing the word Yolŋu (or any other words with a 'ŋ'), you can substitute the letters 'ng' so that Yolŋu looks this: Yolngu.

 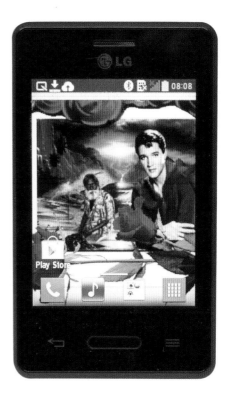

PREFACE

PG   If you reach into your pocket and pull out your phone, what you are holding in your hand is a *nyumuku<u>n</u>iny* [small] thing. It's just a tiny thing, but it's bringing big changes. Just a few years ago no one had a mobile phone. It's a new technology and nowadays we can't leave them alone. They are everywhere in the funeral ground, ceremony ground, hunting, fishing, shopping—everywhere. People are making video calls, watching YouTube, doing Facebook, sending text messages, searching for secondhand *motikas*, doing phone banking and Centrelink *djäma*—all with their phone.

These days we keep the phones close to our bodies. Always, everywhere, together. Any phone: flat ones, any type.

In the old days, Yolŋu went everywhere with their spears. Like my father, up until the '60s or '70s; he always had his spear with him. He used it for hunting, to get food for the family. He used it to protect himself and to show others that he was a man with law and ceremony and connections to the land and environment. These days, every Yolŋu has a phone. Men, women, kids too.

I don't know what will happen in the future for the generations that will follow. I know it's going to be fast, fast, fast. It must be better for their lives, because they will be sitting in the office with everything. You can't run away. Kids will grow up fast with that technology. They'll be in the office, flying on the plane. Even they might fly over to the moon. Because they're catching onto this technology really fast. That's the future. Mobile phones. Computer world. Internet. Google. Kids are learning this fast. Doesn't matter if they're Yolŋu or Japanese.

Is this *yu<u>t</u>a* [new] technology pulling them away from the *wäŋa*, the land of their ancestors? I don't know.

One thing I do know is that Yolŋu can use their phones to do *manymak* [good] things for their family and their future. We know how to use mobile phone technologies in ways that reach further than any Telstra tower. Because sometimes you need to forget about the signal, forget about recharge and concentrate on who you are and where you belong. These days Yolŋu can use the phone to connect us to the *ma<u>d</u>ayin* [sacred objects], the *wäŋa*, the old people, with our sacred patterns and our identity.

This means that there are many *manymak* reasons to hold onto our phones, to keep them in our pockets and our bags, even if sometimes all those calls and messages, beeping, beeping, beeping make you want to throw your phone away. Or smash your SIM card with a rock.

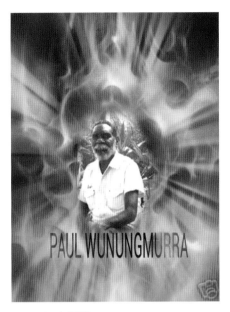

DHALWAŊU FIRE
Kayleen Djingadjingawuy Waṉambi, 2016

This is what I look like on the inside—and this is what it looks like inside the land. We are the same. I am showing myself in a Yolŋu way.

That fire makes my land a dangerous place. Ziggy Gurrumuru is what we call it, because the knife comes out of *gurtha*, out of the fire. My name comes from this place where the dreaming and the land talks. Gurrumuru. My land is hot, powerful. It's been there for a long time. The *yiki* [knife] comes from that *gurtha*.

Each clan has its own *gamunuŋu* [clay, paint, colours, sacred design] from the land. We've got *miny'tji* [patterns] in our *rumbal* [body]. Because we've got *maḏayin* [sacred designs and objects] and identity. You have to show yourself with your body, who you are, your body, your identity... and people will see and straight away know who you are. That *gamunuŋu* gives out the knowledge and wisdom.

My *gamunuŋu* comes, I believe, from my Grandfather's body, and the land itself. It reflects from the water, and the land, and the ancestors. There might be different *dhäwu*, different stories, about this that come from different Yolŋu, but what I believe is that these patterns come from the bottom of the earth, soil, and they hold us firm.

PAUL GURRUMURUWUY

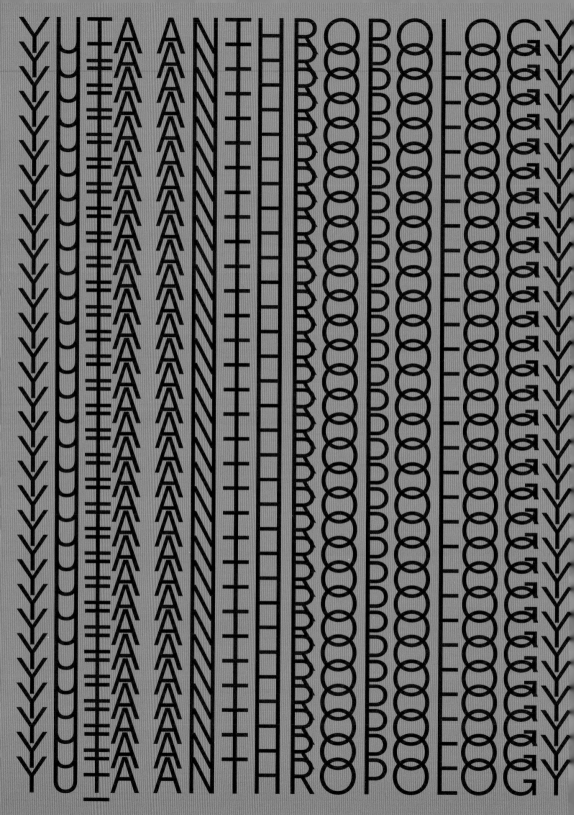

YUTA ANTHROPOLOGY

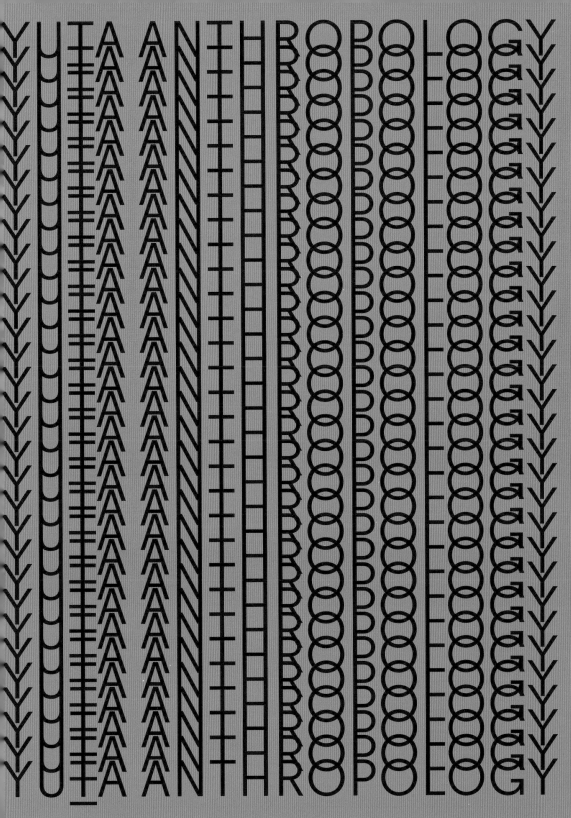

YUTA ANTHROPOLOGY

YU_TA ANTHROPOLOGY

EG   *Balanda* look at the world and see a person there and a tree over there and they see them as separate. That's so boring!

PG   This book is about reconciliation. But our way is different to marching in the street.

                                    ▪

JD   Let's start by affirming the pleasures of play, association, and canny recognition: the way the world can be reconfigured and made anew through deliberate acts of combination and recombination.

      The sorrow and the worry will claim their place in due course, but it will be different to the hand-wringing moralising commonly expressed by *balanda* [non-Aboriginal people] who cannot see past the inertia, fragmentation and loss: the many politicians, bureaucrats, academics, nurses and teachers; all those many concerned visitors and remote-area residents with whom I so often find myself in anxious agreement. This, despite my Yolŋu friends' insistence that the foundations of their patterned world of kinship will always be there, drawing them home.

                                    ▪

JD   If I had to boil this book down to one sentence, it might be this: my Yolŋu friends and family use mobile phones as a technology with which to tap into—and amplify—the push-and-pull of life.

      The Yolŋu phone-made media that we share in this book do more than simply show relationships; they create connections and make old ones anew. Through cheeky acts of recombination, old forms are given new life, and the social order laid down by the actions of ancestral beings is not merely reproduced, but energised and recast, so that new cartographies of the contemporary come into view. Through such processes, worlds once distinct and separate are linked together, though never as a seamless whole.

      In keeping with this performative ethos, *Phone & Spear* mixes together images, stories and voices to create an anthropology of relationship-making. Or, as we call it, *yuṯa* anthropology.

JD   In the Aboriginal languages of east Arnhem Land, *yuṯa* means new. *Yuṯa* anthropology is the term that my friend, colleague and adoptive father, Paul Gurrumuruwuy, uses to describe our decade-long shared experiment with form, image and voice. There is at once shrewd precision, playful provocation and genuine good will in his use of this term. By describing our work as *yuṯa* anthropology, Gurrumuruwuy not only positions himself as an equal alongside me, a university-trained researcher; he also stakes a claim to a discipline, and institutional forms of knowledge, recognition and reward that hold sway far beyond Arnhem Land. The result is a collaboration of an unusual kind: taking the mobile phone as both medium and metaphor for the intensified, technologically mediated connectivity of our times, we offer this book as a shared reflection on—or perhaps, rather, a refraction of—life in a digital age.

Whereas the first wave of mobile phone scholars tended to concentrate on this technology as one revolutionising communication and the 'information landscape', my Yolŋu colleagues and I take up mobile phones as aesthetically potent, world-making devices.[5]

Much has been written about the ways that they connect us in relational spaces that extend beyond our immediate surroundings (at least potentially: as long as our phone is on, in credit and within range of a repeater tower, which is certainly not always the case in Arnhem Land, or even my home office). Carried in intimate proximity in purses and pockets—when not clutched tightly in the hands they are designed for—mobile phones not only increase the already profoundly technological texture of human life, they also create worlds immanent with relationality. With phone in or at hand, at any time and at any moment (again within the limitations of network coverage, battery-life and local protocols), we can be called into sensuous forms of connection with geographically distant people and places. And vice versa. As phones extend our daily communications far beyond the kinds of unmediated face-to-face encounters that many *balanda*, nostalgic for pre-digital days, continue to value above all else, we become newly available to the demands of others, and to the projective trajectories of our own needs, desires and imaginations. In theory, phones mean that we are connectable to anyone, anywhere. But, of course, in practice part of their appeal—and part of their challenge—lies exactly in shaping, and when necessary limiting, our availability to others.

It is this generative tension that animates our book. On the pages that follow, back-and-forth zones of connectivity are examined and activated in multiple registers: between Yolŋu and *balanda*, here and there, now and then, old and new, the living and the dead, the young and the old, the bush and the city, the local and the global. A desire to mediate these spaces of betweenness, while still allowing for distinctiveness and necessary forms of separation, is what gives shape and purpose to *Phone & Spear*.

.

JD If 'old' anthropology understands its task to be revealing one world to another, the challenge of *yuṯa* anthropology is to bring different worlds into relationship.

.

JD Yolŋu often use the term *yuṯa* to describe the distinctive cultural forms and practices that come about when novel or 'foreign' technologies, styles and ideas are taken up in ways that render them pleasurably recognisable in accordance with existing local values, aesthetics and histories. *Yuṯa* is a kind of Yolŋu remix: an art of incorporation by which the new is rendered in relationship to the old; a riffing mode of co-creation fuelled by the improvisational energy and outlook of a *yuṯa* generation. *Yuṯa* is fresh. *Yuṯa* is exciting.

Yuṯa forms refract contemporary life through the prism of *gurruṯu* [kinship relations] and ancestral themes, but without invoking the strict seriousness, depth and danger associated with the *maḏayin* [the 'old', sacred objects and designs controlled by certain senior male clan leaders]. *Yuṯa* music, dance and art enable individuals to express, and to be recognised for, their own creativity as they manifest aspects of their Yolŋu identity. When one creates a *yuṯa* song, image, dance, the new and the old are brought into a relationship of mutuality through creative labour. The old and the new are made co-constitutive: the new renews the old; the old is manifest as the source of the new. In the process the new generation are able to demonstrate their skill, their wit, their dextrous grasp of a here-and-now made thickly resonant across generations. While this description may sound a little earnest, there is often a mischievous, even subversive, bravado to *yuṯa* forms that adds to their allure.

While *yuṯa* styles may enable young people to play around with a free-ing frivolity, there is nothing frivolous in Gurrumuruwuy's conception of *yuṯa* anthropology. He brings the knowledge and authority of a life-time, including a ritually attuned sense of *the enlivening effects of making things new*. He is concerned with something much more substantial, and socially efficacious, than the pleasures of novelty, bricolage and fun (though the exhilaration of having fun also has its place, as we shall see). While some readers may expect that an Indigenous researcher and artist might want to put a defining distance between his work and that of anthropology, this is not how Gurrumuruwuy sees it. As a Yolŋu man in his mid-sixties, he has no interest in unburdening himself of tradi-tions—neither his own, nor mine—in the context of his life, discarding all that has come before in the pursuit of fresh, or alternative, futures makes no sense. Rather, Gurrumuruwuy's vision for *yuṯa* anthropology is compelled by an appreciation for an intrinsic, necessarily two-way relationship between the old and the new. And so, rather than repudiat-ing anthropology for its lingering colonial ties and presumptions, he is interested in the possibilities of renewing this discipline. As am I.

■

JD   There are, of course, pragmatic reasons for casting our work within an already existing framework, one that is readily recognisable to *balanda*. Gurrumuruwuy and his family value our work together as a means of gaining paid employment, travelling the world and accruing forms of social capital that might, eventually, lead to greater financial reward. '*Yuṯa* anthropology can be a way of making our name *yindi* [big],' Gur-rumuruwuy declared as we boarded the plane to attend the Australian Anthropology Society conference in Adelaide. He repeats this ambition when we talk about new projects and the next round of grant applica-tions.

But what actually makes *yuṯa* anthropology 'anthropology' is the fact that it develops, and tests, a theory of social relations (one that has been adapted from a Yolŋu theory of relations, and which includes the more-than-human world of ancestral spirits, land and sea). Through our work, Gurrumuruwuy sees a potential to communicate aspects of Yolŋu life in ways that can be engaging and interesting for *balanda*, while steering clear of revealing 'inside' information about the *maḏayin* and its *dhuyu* [secret-sacred] depths. But, even more fundamentally, he sees this as a chance for his understanding of what it is to be human, to inform—and, perhaps, transform—a discipline established to study just that.

Aesthetics have been central to this task. You hold in your hands a book created as a visual object, an object designed to generate relationships. In crafting *Phone & Spear* we aimed to produce experiential and co-constitutive forms of knowledge. From the outset, we envisaged the book as something that a casual passer-by should be attracted to, and so drawn to pick up and, at the very least, flip through. We combined images and texts with the hope of drawing people further in, activating readers as sensuous, imaginative and feelingful participants in the making of meanings and connections. (Given the importance of images to our approach, you should take the term 'reader' here in a pretty broad sense.) By taking the project of 'writing a book' as an opportunity to work with voice, text, images, patterns and colour, we sought to materialise something vital, alluring and resonant: a relational object capable of engaging readers without any previous interest in, or knowledge of, Yolŋu life.

■

JD   From the outset Gurrumuruwuy and his family have been clear that their aim is to connect with *balanda* audiences. In our choice of language, stories and design we drew from Yolŋu principles as they might be used to engage *balanda*, rather than to communicate directly to Yolŋu. They saw this as a book to be used in universities and beyond, a book that should be capable of simultaneously interesting, informing and moving anyone enticed to pick it up in the first place. Working across media modalities and in different registers of voice, we have been motivated by a series of central questions: *How might we use images—and indeed not just any images, but intimate Yolŋu family portraits—to share feelings with strangers? What might such a project look like? Sound like? What might it achieve?*

Dhäkay-ŋänhawuy rom [the law of feelings] is what Gurrumuruwuy calls aesthetics that guide us. Aesthetics as we mean the term here is concerned with the ways that perception, sensation, imagination and memory play a critical role in constituting particular 'structures of feeling', as Raymond Williams put it. In our formulation, aesthetics is a relational zone of social transformation; the camera and screen become sites for the production and transmission of affect that moves between bodies, human and otherwise, leaving invisible traces and tetherings. 'Sharing

You have to show yourself with your body, who you are, your body, your identity... and people will see and straight away know who you are. That *gamunuŋu* gives out the knowledge and wisdom.

PAUL GURRUMURUWUY

feelings' is how we often describe our anthropological practice in English. We are concerned with what happens when one person's deep feelings become palpable to another, thereby producing, in response, a powerful surge of affect that results in a profound sense of connection: *ŋayaŋu waŋgany* [a state of being united through feeling].

Dhäkay-ŋänhawuy rom, in other words, is affect calibrated to produce a very specific dynamic of feeling. Gurrumuruwuy and his family value such transactions for their intimate and incremental social effects. For, as Yolŋu know, with time and practice, these feelings accumulate on one's *ŋayaŋu*, to become the foundation for an open-hearted capacity to relate to the world and others.

As particular registers of sorrow, love and longing are made to mingle and move between individual bodies, they create closeness and connection. This is the push-and-pull that lies at the heart of this book, and so much of the media we share: a movement from one *ŋayaŋu* to another, a social surge of activated feelings that gradually subsides to coalesce on individual hearts. This then informs the way they subsequently see (and hear and taste and smell and touch) the world.

This practised capacity for *feeling with* provides an essential attunement, a capacity to respond with heart and mind, memory and imagination to a world constantly calling one into relationship.

Through deliberately activating dynamics of feeling and remembering, envisaging and recognising—whether during rituals, while watching TV or walking down a road far from home—members of Miyarrka Media and their families are constantly calling forth, and drawing on, associations with other places and other times. Through these imagistic practices of feeling, they actively render worlds in palpable constellations of relationship. These heartfelt dynamics, in turn, become a means by which to constitute relationships with unfamiliar places and people.

JD   *Yuṯa* anthropology does not arise out of a vacuum. For many decades now there have been sustained efforts on many fronts by Yolŋu and *balanda* dedicated to finding ways to forge meaningful and lasting relationships between two very different knowledge systems, both within and outside formal institutional settings.

As *yuṯa* anthropology brings a combination of Yolŋu and *balanda* perspectives to bear on the methods, forms and ambitions of a discipline that has been at least peripherally part of Yolŋu lives since the 1930s, it draws direct inspiration from earlier anthropologies, including those traditions concerned with aesthetics, the now-established subfields of visual and sensuous anthropology, as well as those whose work has highlighted the performative challenge of evoking affect through writing or audiovisual production. In particular, Faye Ginsburg's seminal thinking about 'embedded aesthetics' and what she has recently described as the 'relational accountability' of Indigenous media highlights the profoundly situated ethical-aesthetic imperatives that animate a wide range of Aboriginal media production, both on-screen and off. Likewise, Eric Michaels' early work with Warlpiri Media in Central Australia has had a lasting influence on my own work by modelling collaborative, practice-led methodologies that allow one to attend to the ways that Aboriginal people might take up the camera and its associated social networks of production and distribution for their own purposes.

Histories of encounter, collaboration and experimentation from Arnhem Land also directly inform this book. *Yuṯa* anthropology has precursors in a history of multimodal ethnographic collaboration with Yolŋu that begins with Donald Thompson's extraordinary photography from the 1930s and 1940s, and that includes the landmark work of Ian Dunlop, Howard Morphy, Pip Deveson, Tom Murray, Jessica de Largy Healy, Aaron Corn and my own earlier work with Warrkwarrkpuyŋu Yolŋu Media, and the late Bäŋgana Wunuŋmurra. While the specific imperatives of Yolŋu social aesthetics and politics have clearly shaped these projects—often involving close friendships and philosophical exchanges between Yolŋu and anthropologists—to my mind, what makes our anthropology *new* is that *Phone & Spear* has been co-authored and co-designed with the explicit ambition of claiming and reconfiguring anthropology's relational potential.

To this end, *yuṯa* anthropology builds upon, and extends, a long-established, and widely practised, Yolŋu strategy of producing intercultural relationships through showing images and objects in the expectation of creating mutuality and regard. However, here images are not expected to do their work alone. Understanding vision as socially generative, and photo assemblage as loving acts of world-making, we crafted these pages ever mindful of the challenges involved in satisfying both Yolŋu and *balanda* regimes of knowledge, understanding *yuṯa* anthropology itself to be inevitably given shape and purpose through the push-and-pull of accountability to distinct and, sometimes, incommensurable worlds.

Repurposing mobile phone media for a new context, we have taken images originally made to circulate within the intimacy of Yolŋu family networks and rendered them capable of calling out to, and sharing stories and feelings with, readers with no prior connection to this material. Rather than an anthropology of art, *Phone & Spear* pursues an artful anthropology: an anthropology that does not expect to extract itself from the circuits of obligation, care and reciprocity through which these images were made to move. Instead we seek to extend these circuits outward, deploying images as agents of social transformation in ways that expand the possibilities of both anthropology and Yolŋu art practice.

On these pages aesthetics is not only inseparable from ethics and politics, it provides the very grounds of analysis, opening up new ways of thinking, a multisensory means by which to address old issues anew. Taking form and content as intimately intermeshed, *yuṯa* anthropology positions our readers as essential participants in the relational fields we cultivate. A Yolŋu aesthetics of meme, remix and recombination provides both energy and analytic force. Through acts of finding, arranging and playfully juxtaposing elements that might appear clumsily kitsch to the untrained eye, we found opportunities to participate in the orchestration, and co-creation, of an ancestrally ordered world of pattern-in-motion that opens itself outwards in a gesture of open invitation.

Within certain limits.

.

JD   Yolŋu hold in their care forms of restricted and specifically owned knowledge that do not easily sync with a digital ethos of open access and creative commons. Fundamental to the very possibility of this book was the willingness of the Yolŋu members of Miyarrka Media to take responsibility for the public release of text and images both now and into the future. Holding family meetings and asking for permission to publish specific images was, perhaps, the easy part. What they have also had to take into account is that circulating stories and images under their own names may lead to future, unforeseeable consequences especially as, once made public and visible in new ways, in new forms, for new audiences, these stories and images cannot be withdrawn. This means that even as Miyarrka Media worked to provide the open-hearted explanations that fill these pages, there has been a countervailing conservatism as we judiciously included only information and images deemed unequivocally suitable for public circulation. We knew that whether or not other Yolŋu care to read the entire text, they would undoubtedly appraise this work with an eye to how we have managed the dynamics of revelation and concealment that are intrinsic to a performative politics of relationally bound knowledge.

In a society that always seeks causal explanations for unexpected death and misfortune, carefully combing over the past to identify transgressions that might have aroused the ire of *galka* [malicious sorcerers], this book potentially leaves my friends and their close family members vulnerable to blame, or even retribution, for what someone might determine to be an improper act of exposure, even though there is nothing at all explicitly sacred or secret in anything we have selected for publication. A few Yolŋu expressed exactly this concern for future personal safety when we showed them what we were up to. When I talked about this with Gurrumuruwuy and his children, they announced that they were not frightened, that they are a different kind of Yolŋu. Gurrumuruwuy was quite insistent that there was no problem with our approach, saying, 'The art in this book is only lite. We are not stealing the *maḏayin*. We are just showing links and patterns.'

■

JD New media theorists, Bolter and Grusin, use the term *remediation* to challenge modernist assumptions that new technologies necessarily entail a break with aesthetic and cultural principles of the past. They identify remediation by pointing to the ways that one media, such as painting, gives rise to the next, say photography. In the process, they argue that the cultural significance of new media lies in the way that they refashion, rival or pay homage to earlier ones. This idea of remediation encourages a critical attention to the role of technology in materialising relationships and histories; it alerts us to cultural forms shaped by back-and-forth relationships that may not immediately be self-evident, especially when shifts of form, practice and technology seem to present evidence of a newness predicated precisely on a radical discontinuity with the past. The concept of remediation, in other words, points towards the performative dimensions of technological innovation. It gestures to the ways in which a generative relationship between the old and the new is activated through the creative labour of repurposing for new contexts and new times.

If remediation brings a focus to formal and technical innovation, a notion of remix (a term commonly used by my colleagues, though with a Yolŋu flavour) allows us to attend to the potential of content gathered from intersecting worlds in motion, alerting us to the relational possibilities created through the work of joining sometimes unlikely things together. In this way, *yuta* anthropology is itself a form of both remediation and remix, *Yolŋu-style*. Informed by anthropological histories, and inspired by the emergent art forms made possible by mobile phones and Google Play, this work of cut-and-paste poetics conducted by an extended Yolŋu family, and the ethnographer they adopted twenty-five years ago, brings together once-distinctly separate ontologies and epistemologies in the hope that Yolŋu and *balanda* societies might be drawn closer. Together we seek to forge shared understandings, even as we each speak from our own, distinctly located, points of view. Gurrumuruwuy describes his vision of coexistence, 'Yolŋu and *balanda*. Together, but not mixed up', thereby refusing a future in which everyone and everything becomes mashed together into compliant—and boring—homogeneity.

As *yuta* anthropology creates its own dynamics of push-and-pull, its own field of generative tension and possibility, it sometimes brings to the fore apparently irreconcilable differences. This is also part of the point: not everything should be translated or can be translated. Nonetheless, we understand that quite a lot of information is necessary if readers are to appreciate the images on something resembling their own terms. In order to thicken the spaces between image, text and reader, we have provided explanations that mix fact, memory, story, analysis and associative thinking. We have carefully chosen what to emphasise and what not to spell out. In this process, my Yolŋu friends tended to make declarative statements, providing glimpses of the information lying within in order to show how personal histories and ancestral actions bind the images together. I tell other kinds of stories, drawing from my own life history and ways of knowing in an effort to make these images—and the ideas, lives, histories and feelings that infuse them—palpable and inviting to the hearts of strangers.

Approaching images as affective agents, understanding vision as socially generative, and taking assemblage as a loving act of world-making, we have together created a visual anthropology that reaches beyond observation and, indeed, the manifestly visible; a visually driven engagement with the world concerned with praxis, processes and relationships; an artful anthropology energised by repetition and juxtaposition, rather that things that stand alone. There's a cunning to such work, and an openness too, in that it refuses to accede to an oppositional politics that would impose, and police, boundaries between 'black' and 'white'.

Phone & Spear is a book that performs its argument: it does not simply analyse relations, it seeks to make them. In doing so, it offers something more than a collaboratively written, community-authorised account of an Indigenous lifeworld—our purview is broader, our aims more inclusive and our methods have felt more risky. None of us can know how the book will be received, or what others might actually take away from these pages. But whatever comes of this shared experiment inspired by mobile phones and the creative forms they enable, we are confident that *Phone & Spear* contributes something new: not a catalogue of difference, nor an archive of the already gone, but a poem to the push-and-pull of relationships, an ode to shared futures, yet to be found.

If 'old' anthropology understands its task to be revealing one world to another, the challenge of *yuṯa* anthropology is to bring different worlds into relationship.

JENNIFER DEGER

DHÄKAY-ŊÄNHAWUY ROM DHÄKAY-ŊÄNHAWUY ROM

DHAKAY-ŊÄNHAWUY ROM DHAKAY-ŊÄNHAWUY ROM

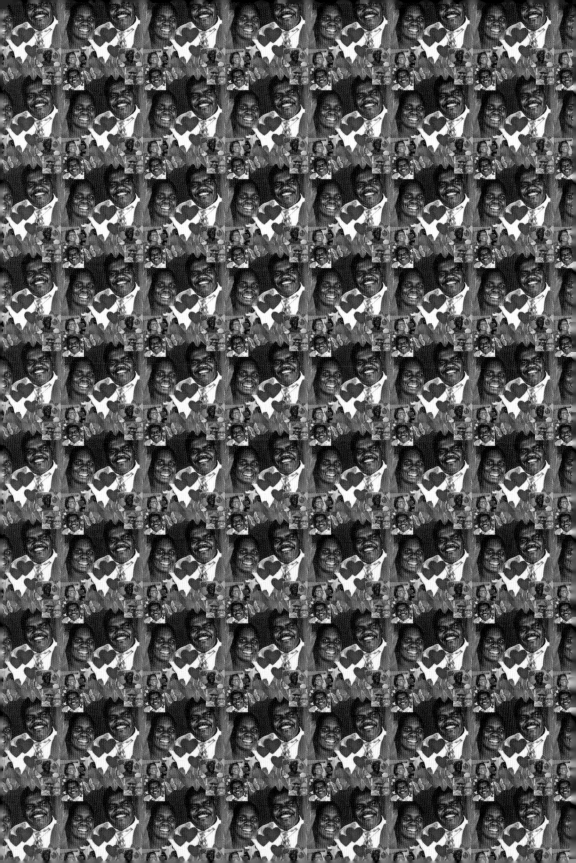

DHÄKAY-ŊÄNHAWUY ROM

PG　*Dhäkay-ŋänhawuy rom* means 'sharing feelings'. Or maybe we could call it 'the law of feelings', or maybe there's a better way to say it in English. What I'm talking about is that experience of connection that you can get through feelings. That's what we are doing here. Sharing feelings from inside us and giving them to you. So you can feel and you can know.

Dhäkay-ŋänhawuy rom means that you can feel something just by looking at us and hearing the *dhäwu* [stories] we are giving out. These feelings come from inside us and they can go inside you.

We are sharing what we've got, sharing with our experiences, our bodies, our *ŋayaŋu*. And when someone does that, other people can see and other people can take it in. Then they can see and feel the same thing that we've got.

When you feel inside then you cry, because it hits you right in your *ŋayaŋu*, and then it comes out and you cry... you feel sorrow, what we call *warwuyun*, or you feel happy, like you feel satisfied from the richness of that feeling.

Dhäkay-ŋänhawuy rom means when that feeling goes in and comes out it shows in your reaction. Something happens inside and other people can see. Other people can feel it as well. Your body opens up; that's the connection. That feeling, it sits on your *ŋayaŋu*, *doturrk* [heart] and your *djäl* [your desire]. And it comes out from your body... then you cry and you show and people can feel for themselves how you feel.

You don't need to speak or understand Yolŋu *matha* [language, tongue], because you can feel it, straight away. If *balanda* can take in those feelings, it would help them a lot.

EG　*Dhäkay* means taste. That's what we're talking about. Because when you get this taste you want more and more. It's delicious.

For example, if you watch Jennifer take a sip of wine, she always moves it around in her mouth, right to the back of her mouth. She does it every time. Tasting it. If you watch her face you know that she is tasting all that flavour. The she takes the next sip. Because it's delicious. She wants more.

PG　Some people are *gumurr-däl* [hard-chested]. They keep their heart closed.

But sometimes *dhäkay-ŋänhawuy rom* works. For soft-hearted people, especially. When you feel it, your body will show you. Your outside body will show your reaction; it comes from your heart but your *rumbal* [body] will show whether you cry, whether you are connected with that feeling. Sometimes it just hits. Boom! Drawing you near where you belong, drawing you nearer to who you are. It is in the *manikay*, in the songs and the stories.

Dhäkay-ŋänhawuy rom is just giving out and sharing... and then those feelings settle down. That *dhäkay-ŋänhawuy rom* settles down on your heart, and it is there, all the time. Like it's waiting and when the moment comes, it is there, filling you up... the same attitude and feeling is there. It's powerful. And it is through that feeling that you and I can be connected, from inside me to inside you. Alive in us both, it draws us together, even though we are living different lives in different places, we can share feelings together.

Young people, they don't really feel it. They can't really, they are too young. But when you get to a certain age, then you *can* feel it, especially older people from twenty-five and up to thirty, that's the age when their reactions change, their *muḻkurr* [heads] change (because young people have different things on their mind and heart).

Anger is another *djäma*. Jealousy is different again, a different reaction. With what we are talking about here with *dhäkay-ŋänhawuy rom*, the feelings are only sorrow or worry or that feeling of happiness that you can get. As you get older you get more knowledge, more memories... and more feelings, from going to ceremonies, spending time at *bäpurru* [funerals]. The *wäŋa* has the same *rom*. The *wäŋa* will feel you and it will talk to you. The *dharpa* [trees], the *wäŋa*, the sea. It's a *yindi* [big, important] word. I am talking at this level, but it goes it down, down, deep to your *djäl* and *ŋayaŋu*.

It's there all the time; it doesn't matter that *balanda* came, it doesn't change the feelings.

Dhäkay means taste. That's what we're talking about. Because when you get this taste you want more and more. It's delicious.

ENID GURUŊULMIWUY

CAN A BOOK HUM? CAN A BOOK HUM?

CAN A BOOK HUM? CAN A BOOK HUM?

CAN A BOOK HUM?

PG   Can you remember life without mobile phones? Nowadays we see these little things everywhere. In the city, in the bush, hunting or at circumcision ceremonies... young people, old people, everyone has one. It's a different life now. You have a phone in your pocket, I have one in mine.

If I had your number, I could ring you up. Just like that. Anytime, anywhere. It wouldn't matter if you are Chinese or Indian or American. If I had enough credit, I could dial your number and hear your voice, maybe live, maybe on your message bank. Does this mean we're all connected? I don't know. Maybe you wouldn't pick up because you don't recognise my number. Maybe you're tired, or stressed, or busy. Maybe you're interested, or maybe you're scared of unknown callers.

If you did answer my call, what would we say to each other?

                                    ▪

JD   Can a book hum?

This is not a literal question, although it might be taken for one in a context where humans are not the only ones who cry, growl and shudder; in places where bees hum and dance and worry for the dead; where stony outcrops and other sacred sites may be heard to boom with sorrow or the furious reprimand of the old people, those ancestral spirits who, given half a chance, will find ways to take the living to task for what they have failed to do, or look after, or themselves become. Other times, those same places, those same spirits, will give plentiful fish and game, welcoming kin with generous recognition; they'll participate in rituals, whisper songs to the sleeping or flicker to life in a photograph, embodying both the source and the emergent force of creation. It is these potent and often scary places, and the images, spirits and stories that inhere within them, that remain the grounds of Yolŋu power, identity and futures.

PG   Many Yolŋu people these days use their phones to make family *bitja* and to record videos. This didn't used to happen, this kind of picture-making, but now we're in a global world. Through the phone you can see the *yindi* picture; that big picture is telling you the story of the land, all the places, belonging to you. Through the phone you can connect to your country, to your family.

We want to surprise you with our mobile phone *bitja* and our stories. To make you interested and to draw you close. So you might recognise us and connect to us, through feelings and imaginations, through the images we make on our phones, even though you are sitting all the way over there, somewhere, wherever you belong, *barrkuwatj* [separate, far away].

Our work is here to get that *dhäwu* [story] down, in the *djorra'* [book], in black and white. Together with all those colours and patterns we're showing you. This is a new way to share Yolŋu life.

Yolŋu people don't care about writing. But *balanda* people read and read. That's how we'll catch them. Like when that honey is in the tree... that's how we're going to make this book.

■

JD Can a book hum?

The notion of a humming book first came to me after struggling to find a textual form adequate to the digital lives and materialities that are the subject of *Phone & Spear*. I liked the way it pointed straight to the challenge: how to mediate the multiple many spaces of betweenness that shape our work? How to animate the gaps between words and images, digital and analogue, English language and Yolŋu concepts, between past and present, past and future, us and them, here and there...? How to set up a field of resonance between worlds coming ever more into relation, and yet, still, distinctly far apart?

■

JD Can a book hum?

On the phone one day, I put my question to Gurrumuruwuy. He got it immediately. And ran with it. Straight to bees and hives.

PG Humming? *Yo* [yes]. Humming. Like harmony. That sort of thing? *Yo*, that's what we're doing. Making it one voice, one *rirrakay*, humming with unity, with *waŋgany* [one] feeling. That makes me think about someone who hums like *guku*, like the bush bees, and the honey. When you are searching for honey, you have to put your head close to the tree so you

LIKE HONEY FROM HEAVEN
Simeon Rigamawuy Wunuŋmurra, 2010

GUKU
Kayleen Djingadjingawuy Waṉambi, 2015

Waṉambi people are the Honey Bee people. Mum always called herself *djiwarrpuy guku*. That means 'honey from heaven'. My brother made this after she died.

See those flowers, they are like the flowers on the *gaḏayka*' tree that attract the bees. The green colour is to show her *märi* from Wangurri people.

MEREDITH BALANYDJARRK

These are the Honey Bee people. The *guku* [honey] shows the children called Larrak. They are the current and future generations. Everything fits together.

Because that honey holds everything.

KAYLEEN DJINGADJINGAWUY

can hear that sound, that hum of those bees. *Rrambaṇi*, together, *yaka* [not] back and forth. But inside. Together. Alive!

JD He directed me to go back and look at the video footage from the day of his wife's burial, fourteen days after we had brought her back to Gapuwi-yak from the morgue.

PG Look at the footage from the room beginning from when we get ready to bring the coffin out. In the beginning of that clan *manikay*, in that part of the song, that *guku*, the honey bees and eggs, are humming *yothu* and ŋä<u>ndi</u>, the children and the mother together. Not like later when those bees go in and out, not when they're dancing, but when they bring that coffin and they sit with the leaves and hum, everything together. *Waŋga-ny*. As one. Mother and child. We see them like that as *guku*, the honey and the flowers and the bees, the pollen, the eggs and that honey-hunting ancestor too. All together.

JD Straight to humming bees and assemblages of aliveness; straight to a poetics of attraction, connection and co-creation.

·

JD Looking back at the footage, I remembered the way that hum moved through my body that day, voices rising and cross-cutting, clapsticks beating, sonic field disrupting boundaries between inside and out, to create an encompassing field of sensuous connection that held us all, everyone becoming one, becoming *waŋgany* around that coffin, the social orchestrated in patterns of kinship based on *yothu-yindi* patterns of mother and child: social patterns given form by ancestral action and given depth and meaning through individual life histories, the hum giving voice to a sense of shared purpose and connection, experienced through the quiver of affect, memory, story and love.

Positioned in this way, brought alive by all these registers, my humming book metaphor also took shape within a specific set of relationships. Drawing on his authority as *djuŋgaya*, or ritual manager, for Marraŋu people and their *guku*, Gurrumuruwuy located my own work within the same kind of *yothu-yindi* ancestrally ordered relationships that had held us all together in that room.

PG That's what you have to write, *gäthu* [daughter], bring your *muḻkurr* [mind] and *ŋayaŋu* [heart] to the *djäma*. Concentrate, find the right words. We want *balanda* to understand how deep and how far Yolŋu can see and feel with these little phones. I want them to see how smart our kids are. How they use the phone to connect to the land and the old people. Only you know how to do the writing part. Make it hum.

■

JD Michael Taussig sees humming as 'central to language, humming being neither conscious or unconscious, neither singing nor saying, but rather the sound where the moving mind meets the moving body...' Like Gurrumuruwuy, he encourages us to tune into humming as an act of emergence.

The buzz of collectives in action.
The echo and vibration of worlds coming into relationship.
Hum as sign, and sound, of life.

In this rendering, the hum is not a totalising aesthetic. It does not reduce everything to a singularity, or undifferentiated mass. Instead, it affirms the spaces of separation through which resonance claims its relational hold. It orchestrates, in short, a generous kind of unity.

■

JD Listening again to the video of Yangathu's funeral, I hear the lead singers 'finding the tune' as they say, in the moments before they begin. The *djirrikay* leads the singing, his voice rising as he calls the sacred names, the clapsticks marking the rhythm, other younger voices joining in response, the small room keeping us tightly together, intensifying the visceral echo.

I remember the power and the tenderness of at moment as we lifted the white coffin that had been specially covered with white fluff—the colour of the bee larvae—and took her outside, everyone assembled knowing that they were looking at a felled tree, split open with its hive exposed and the bees moving back and forth, knowing they must leave it behind and find another home, yet reluctant to leave, moving back and forth, between the tree—their mother, their womb—and a future without her.

PG   When you chop down the tree you can hear those bees flying around with the same *rirrakay*, the same sound, not high and low, but the same.

       Yothu-yindi [child and mother], Dhaḻwaŋu and Marraŋu tribes. It doesn't matter if you are young or old. One sound, one feeling, one meaning.

JD   Maybe, then, it's more than resonance I hear in this hum?
       Maybe it's the sound of separation filled with the possibility of connection? Maybe it's the sound of joining together?

                                    ▪

JD   Is my job as anthropologist simply put my ear to the tree? To listen and transcribe as people talk about ancestral bees, honey-hunting ancestors, creation and mobile phones? Should my Yolŋu colleagues' task be simply to translate and patiently explain?

                                    ▪

PG   This is a little project, but a lot of work. We have to go slowly. We have to make it clear. So that you can understand, even though I know it is hard for *balanda*. It is hard to understand what we are telling you now. What we are showing you. But keep going. There are riches here. That's why we are working together. Polishing it all up. Bit by bit.

                                    ▪

JD   Although Miyarrka Media is based in Gapuwiyak, none of us actually live there permanently. We live 'scattered'—as Gurrumuruwuy says, using the English word—residing in, and moving between, a number of outstations, communities and cities in northern Australia. We remain in constant, almost daily, contact via phone and phone-transmitted images and texts (but never use social media platforms). We worked on this project together in intense bursts in Gapuwiyak, Darwin and Cairns. We also travelled together to Brisbane, Sydney, Adelaide, and New York for exhibitions, screenings, and talks.

PG   We might be *barrkuwatj*, our team might come from separate places with different thinking, living in different, different places, like the outstation and the city, but we can make one picture.

．

JD   Phones mark the passing of time in dizzying ways. Early on I returned from a field trip determined to throw out everything I'd written up to that point because it felt so clumsy and outdated. Such was the speed of change. Not just in terms of the technologies themselves, but in the ways in which Yolŋu are taking up, and responding to, the new kinds of digital connectivity enabled by the mobile phones, tablets and laptops, which are becoming increasingly integral to the pressures, pleasures and contingencies of Yolŋu life. Even in the media we do address, a stain of time—an invitation to nostalgia—creeps across images that once, not so long ago, struck us as so very fresh and new. The muted colours and grainy pixelation of 3gp files announce themselves as images from another era. Videos from only five years ago look ancient: the pixelated blurriness, the slight syncopation in the replay. This makes us feel somehow more tender towards these images, seized as they are from the flow of time.

But, as I keep reminding myself, if on one level this subject can be characterised by its speed and change, at another level it's about increments of understanding that can only accrue with time. Everything I know that really matters about these worlds comes out of a locatable history; I can track an unfolding of attachment and realisation through things that have happened with certain people, in certain places, over what now feels like a very long time. And so, more than I ever could have anticipated when I began, back in the days of analogue, my work depends on connections forged in specific moments—and the ways that these connections become tempered by time.

In this rendering time is neither steady nor strictly linear. Lives are made and marked by moments and events, stories and images. Energies and intensities rise, and then they fall away. There's a certain rhythm (though the beat is unpredictable); there's a sense that things return, not to repeat themselves exactly, but to create echoes that loosely hold things together.

Life as rhythmic evanescence. The hum of time.

MAKING THINGS LIVELY MAKING THINGS LIVELY

MAKING THINGS LIVELY MAKING THINGS LIVELY

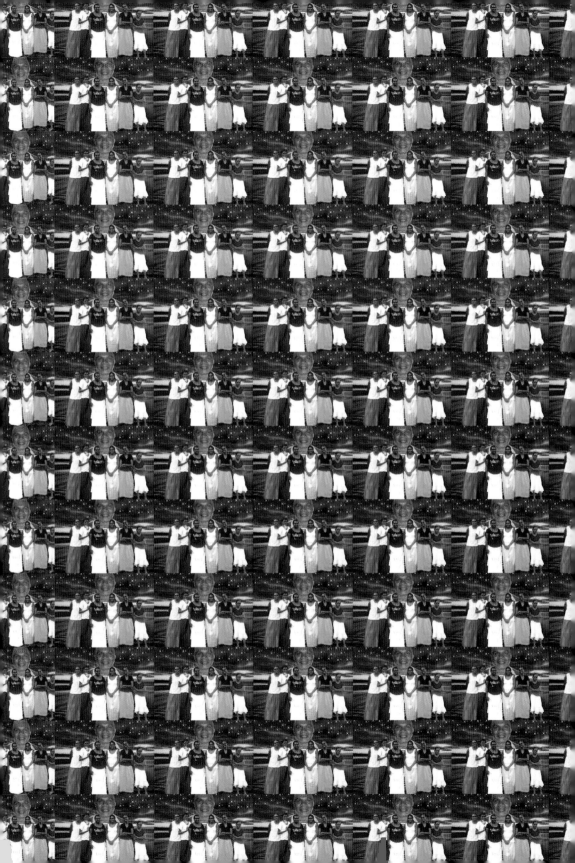

MAKING THINGS LIVELY

In 2008, the introduction of Telstra's 3G mobile-network gen-
erated a wave of creative energy across the bush communities
of Arnhem Land. New genres of video, photography and perfor-
mance flourished. Travelling lightning-speed via satellite and
Bluetooth, this digital culture rode the energy of the new and the
cheeky. Moving hand-to-hand, kin-to-kin, community-to-com-
munity, it drew inspiration from both the Internet and the ances-
tral. It was made to be watched, to be shared, and then deleted to
make way for the next. So began a new era in Australian Indige-
nous media, a period of intensified communication and creativity
in which phones provided access to new, multimedia vectors of
connection, and, in so doing, enabled Yolŋu to take their place in
an increasingly digital world.

JD I wrote these words a few years ago for the catalogue of an exhibition of mobile phone media curated with my Miyarrka Media colleagues. They catch something of the excitement we wanted to convey—the sense of the speed, the energy of the new, the pleasure Yolŋu found in the young people's self-confident wielding of what they often still refer to as '*balan-da* technologies'.

Right from the early days of the blocky Nokias, and long before smart-phones and social media apps, my Yolŋu friends and family used rudi-mentary, pay-as-you-go phones purchased from the local store to put these relational dynamics into play at an aesthetic register. Personalised ringtones created from snippets recorded at ceremonies were used to orchestrate a deeper call to connection, to project themselves back to country, and so activate the forms of identity and belonging that are the foundation of Yolŋu *rom* [ancestral law]. My friends would describe to me how when they heard their ringtone, they could, for instance, feel the wind, or hear the sea birds calling. They immediately felt themselves to be back amongst family and the spirits of the land. In this way, they used their phones to not only locate themselves within specific constellations of relationships, but to acknowledge the draw of country as the locus of an ancestrally ordered sense of belonging, each time the phone rang.

Later came phones with cameras and, later still, phones with Internet access and touchscreens. For most Yolŋu this was the first time that they had access to the means to make, edit and circulate digital imagery (and of course to view, download and remix images made by others).

.

JD   Initially at my urging, but with a growing sense of shared purpose and pleasure, we collected and curated material for the exhibition that became *Gapuwiyak Calling: Phone-made media from Aboriginal Australia*. We installed it, in various guises, in national and international museums and galleries. We designed the show hoping to stir an interest in strangers, not only through our use of a variety of new media, but the transformative possibilities of the new itself.

Gapuwiyak Calling enacted a call to relationship offered with an openness and optimism that I have come to see as distinctly Yolŋu. From the very first we wanted to 'share Yolŋu life', not to display 'Yolŋu culture'. This formulation, arrived at by Gurrumuruwuy and his family and prominently announced in the introductory wall texts of our exhibitions, emphasises the ways in which my colleagues have continually chosen to position our work as an invitation to engage in forms of experiential encounter, rather than as a project in which difference becomes the defining—and so distancing—conceptual framework.

This phone-made media made the playful and creatively elaborated qualities of Yolŋu life visible like never before. Locating individuals within patterned worlds of connection, they showed how Yolŋu see in overlaid biographical, historical and ancestral patterns of relationship, revealing attachments that anthropological kinship charts—or, for that matter, bark paintings—simply cannot. With their pixel-smudged charm and a look-you-straight-in-the-eye confidence, they offered new ways for others to appreciate the resilient values and imaginative urgencies of life, *Yolŋu-style*.

Yet, despite our best efforts, very few people appreciated *Gapuwiyak Calling* on these terms. The imagery remained too dense—too strange and yet too familiar—for others to *see*, much less love in the ways we do. It was only when the Yolŋu curators were able to talk in more depth with visitors in the gallery that we felt that we'd managed to communicate something of the real value, meaning and purpose of the images we'd put on display. Sometimes these discussions culminated in a warm hug between strangers. Sometimes museum visitors cried.

These encounters and the unexpected tears that flowed from them greatly encouraged our experiment with *dhäkay-ŋänhawuy rom* and cemented our desire to write a book that shares these images with the world on their own terms. In the process of assembling the commentaries, permissions and design, we've also had a chance to draw breath and ask questions, to dwell a little longer with the tensions, as well as the satisfactions and new social horizons, that mobile phones, and the media they circulate, bring forth.

■

PG These days we sit in our little communities in Arnhem Land and we can see what is going on around the world. All through the phone.

■

JD The view of Gapuwiyak from Google Earth is too still, too quiet and too distant, no matter how close I zoom. You can't hear the crows, the diesel motors, the gasp of air conditioners pushed to the limit. You can't smell the dry season fires, or the forty-eight-dollar-a-pack cigarettes inhaled with urgent pleasure. You can't hear the TVs, the video games, the snoring, the sneezing and the asthmatic coughs, the skinny dogs, the squeal of barefoot kids, or the laughter tickled loose by drawn-out stories and giant cups of sweet tea. You can't see those mobile phones everywhere. You can't hear them ringing.

What also elude the satellite-eye view are the ways that Yolŋu increasingly find communities like this uncomfortable places to live. Though it depends who you talk to, I have a sense of growing dissatisfaction and disquiet. The people I know best describe Gapuwiyak and neighbouring Yolŋu communities as dangerous and judgemental; as places where the youth have lost their sense of direction and purpose, where kinship and the structures of relationship that underpin all social relations are becoming frayed; a place where malicious sorcery causes the death of young people. Phones play their part in this too.

When Gurrumuruwuy and his family are in Gapuwiyak (not in the city or his outstation Yalakun), they live at Lot 68. A concrete-brick house with two bedrooms, lime-coloured walls and an unfenced yard, it's been his family home since Yolŋu first settled down in Gapuwiyak. Long-time residents, both *balanda* and Yolŋu, still call it the Yellow House, although these days it is painted green, at Gurrumuruwuy's request. This is the colour of his mother's mother's clan. His *märi*. This is the house where Gurrumuruwuy's wife, Yangathu, gave birth to her youngest daughter Barradakanbuy, in the shower, not realising she was pregnant (she nick-named her the Coke-can baby, for her size and the red colour that links her to the Dhalwaŋu clan of her father); the house is in the same place as his father's camp when Gapuwiyak was first settled in 1968 by mission-aries and Yolŋu working together to establish a timber mill; the house where we held the body of his wife, Yangathu, for more than a week before flying her to Yalakun for burial.

Yolŋu sometimes describe the intergenerational change they are experi-encing in terms of 'losing culture'. However, paying attention to how they speak provides clues to understanding what's at stake. In these discus-sions the powerful and constitutive role of the senses often comes into sharp focus. For instance, Bäŋgana Wunuŋmurra, the first Yolŋu man I collaborated with, characterised the threat of foreign media in terms of a cumulative assault on the sensorium. As he described it, music and film from elsewhere threatened to make Yolŋu *deaf* and *blind* to their own songs and the communicative call of their land. For this reason, he said, it was crucial to make a video that would stimulate 'Yolŋu ways of seeing'. Likewise, when Gurrumuruwuy tells me that one reason he is in-terested in making new media and exhibitions is because 'our culture is fading', he is talking about how colour, sounds and images can stimulate a sensorium that extends beyond human bodies to include a sentient landscape populated by spirits of generations past. The media we share in this book are likewise concerned with the power of perception, in-novation, sensuous stimulation. And the work of assembling the Yolŋu world in relation to what Gurrumuruwuy and others call *the big picture*.

∙

JD When we started, I imagined that the book would be structured in a di-alogic manner, arranged as a kind of critical exchange between myself and other members of Miyarrka Media. However, how we have arranged the texts is not dialogic. Our discussions did not unfold in the order they appear here. And this, again, is part of the point.

As far as my Yolŋu collaborators are concerned, the images, songs and performances that inspire this book already tell their own stories. Gurrumuruwuy's instructions were to the point: 'It's all about colour, and pattern, and making things lively'. In other words, our methods must be aesthetic; texts and images have to work together to produce feelings.

This became even clearer as we went about selecting screenshots from GIFS, slideshows and videos to include. A process of muting and stilling that made me worry that we might be killing the very things we loved. We lost so much: the sound and the movement, the lyrics, the tunes, the jaunty beats. We surrendered the glow and super-saturated colour, the tactility too—that ability to select and move, to resize with our fingers—not to mention the capacity to instantly send on to others. But perhaps above all, we lost the glorious malleability of it all: the sense that one image begets the next.

At this point I realised that *Phone & Spear* might provide an opportunity to experiment not just with the relationship between text and image, but with the production of text *as* image. While still writing and assembling the words, we asked the young designers who had worked on the New York exhibition of *Gapuwiyak Calling* to help us see what this might look like. From there on in, writing the text and designing the layout happened in tandem. Words and images alike needed a poetic approach: an attention to rhythm and to repetition; for repetition, as Yolŋu know, need not deaden with its sometimes-rote insistence. Repetition can be the source of life itself, recursive creativity can enable processes of renewal. And so, the making of this book became a shared and loving labour of playful pattern-making. Rather than seeing it as a purely writing exercise, I began to treat the curation of texts also as a form of assemblage (in the old-fashioned art sense).

In order to find our hum, we had to generate a multilayered aesthetics of resonance—across media, across generations, across cultures and across individual differences. It had to hold us all, and to satisfy us all: in spite—or, maybe, exactly because of—our differences. So, as well as recording and transcribing the input from my Yolŋu colleagues, I sought to intercut, and even interrupt, my own written analysis and stories. Not wanting difference to be denied, or otherwise overcome, we claimed our differences as manifestly integral to the very possibility of resonance.

That is how *Phone & Spear* became something more than a project of polyvocal ethnography. It became a shared experiment with *book as*

Here I am dancing at my father's funeral, showing myself as Wurrumba with a shark liver in my mouth. The fat tells about the *waku* born from Gurruwiwi people.

The four sharks represent the mother Wurrumba. Wurrumba lives in the clear, shallow water. That water calls himself *gapu ḏarrtjalk*. Underneath this water lives Witij, the rainbow serpent. If you watch carefully, when you see that shark moving in the water you will see the rainbow colours.

The stars here are the glistening water, the same effect as the light that dapples and shines on the shark's head from the water.

The fat represents the *yothu*. At funerals the mothers of that person who's passed away will have that fat painted on their bellies, around their belly button.

If they need to fight then Gälpu people call themselves Wurrumba. They show themselves as an angry shark. Becoming Wurrumba like that lifts you up to be a hero. It pumps you up. It makes you ferocious. Powerful.

WARREN BALPATJI

This one is beautiful to me. From a distance, especially, it looks like *maḏayin*—that's our sacred possessions and our deep and secret knowledge. If you look close up you can see myself and my sister, together with our two brothers, who have passed away. But the way Yolŋu can see it, we are not sitting there alone. All of life is there. Stories, songs, ceremonies, feelings, movement... the richness of life.

In ceremony, the *ḏalkarra* who leads the singing calls the special names of our country; it brings old people bubbling up, out of the water to be with us. Through the ceremony we flow together. You can feel the old people, you can even see them standing there amongst us. And that's what I see here, in this *bitja*. There's deep meaning bubbling up here. More pattern, deeper feeling, more connection. This is where we come from. And this is how we live.

The first time I saw that kind of *bitja djäma*, I thought 'wow'! When we put this altogether, it's like talking to you. But only through outside pictures. Through photos and that kind of stuff like frames and colours that the kids find on the Internet.

But, still, through the colour and patterns the old people can see more, they can see deeper, they can see the *maḏayin* and all the connections that an image like that can hold. Old people are smart up here, you know.

These patterns bring out more energy; our bodies are connecting to the land and sea.

PAUL GURRUMURUWUY

When you see a pattern from a long way away, it catches your eye. It makes you come close. Like this pattern now. First you might see only the pattern and the colour, you might stop and think, this is lovely, or this is full of energy, but when you look closer you can see the people, the stories, the deep connections. If you come really close then you can see everything. It pulls you in.

This one now has more meaning and more connections by bringing in the Marraṇu people with their honey and bees. I'm the *djuŋgaya* for this clan. We're connected through the land and through my own mother too.

My kids call Marraṇu mother, they have responsibilities for this ceremony. This is how we live. Not just one way. *Balanda* live only one way, they have only a small family, like with mum and dad and kids, brothers and sisters, maybe grandma and grandpa. But Yolŋu got more relationships. Our family spreads out. Out and out.

Looking at this picture you can see all the life. Spreading out and going deep.

PAUL GURRUMURUWUY

gamunuŋgu, an experiment that takes pattern as the source of life and futures, a form with a fluctuating pulse and patterns works to hold us all as *waŋgany* by drawing from stories, images, disparate ambitions, interwoven lives, hidden agendas, not to mention sacred knowledge withheld. All this remixed in a humming space that allows for both resonance and dissonance: the push-and-pull of life and kinship intensified to encompass sameness and difference, past and present, here and there, Yolŋu and *balanda*, sorrow and deep, satisfied happiness.

PG *Yo* [yes], you can see this book like *gamunuŋgu*. It's just another way of telling stories.

            ■

PG Sometimes I think that what we are trying to do here with all these *bitja* and *dhäwu* might be too much. Too much for *balanda* to understand. But I want to get it clear so that people everywhere, even in the States or Germany or Japan, anyone can understand. That's my aim. That's why we've worked so hard on this book. Polishing up these *dhäwu*. Giving you the story and the picture. As clear as we can. Every picture, Dhuwa and Yirritja, we have to give a clear picture to *balanda*. That's why we're doing this *djäma*, this work.

  At the same time, we need to keep those Yolŋu back at home happy. We can only use the *bitja* if everyone agrees. We want them to feel proud. Because with this book these *bitja* can be there for a long time. Maybe the next generations might be interested. Maybe they will read this book.

  Some Yolŋu might be nervous about doing this kind of work. Because it is a responsibility, everyone can see that you are showing the world something new.

            ■

EG We need to ask people to use these *bitja*. We need authorisation. Otherwise people are going to ask, who's doing these things?

PG You can't just talk roughly when it comes to things like this, sometimes talking over the phone won't work. You have to make it straight, so family will agree to give these pictures to our project. That's why I had to fly over to other communities, and sit down with family there, so that everyone can understand.

Otherwise there might be a fight at the card game, or bad feelings coming up. Some Yolŋu might be frightened to do this kind of work. But my family, we like it. I am used to this kind of *djäma*.

EG We are proud. We want to share. We are putting anthropology through a Yolŋu *djalkiri* [foundation, anchor].

PG Most other Yolŋu won't care about this book, they'll just have a look and throw it away. But *balanda* will want this because it is new, new pattern, new *dhäwu*, new... where it's coming from. Not like the anthropology from the 1980s or 1990s. It will make *balanda* excited.

Even museums, or government departments, or universities will want this because from here you can explore more and more. Because *balanda* like to concentrate. Tourists can grab that book and go home and read. And with that book they can make a decision about where to go next, to explore this kind of information in a deeper way...

EG *Matharamamirr*. That means like peeling a fruit, or scaling a fish.

■

JD Sometimes we talk the about the 'old days', back in the 1990s, when Gapuwiyak and its surrounding outstations felt happier, less chaotic. Gurrumuruwuy's children describe how they grew up at a time when everyone fitted together: 'people were not running in whatever direction they felt like'. They worry that Yolŋu are becoming like *balanda* because they are ignoring the *rom*.

They complain that people today are only following their own *djäl*, or desire.

■

EG With this book *balanda* will get feelings that will make them come *bala-räli*. They will read and be drawn close. Yolŋu and *balanda* will have to recognise each other.

JD   When an outsider moves to a Yolŋu community they find themselves, if they are open to it, drawn into relationships that turn on the twinned possibility of mutuality and difference. (Such invitations are by no means exclusive to anthropologists.) On being adopted one is always positioned in a matrix of relationships that runs across time and space. You are invited to become *wangyangy* with Yolŋu, and people will choose to see you that way, within the patterning of kinship and obligation, even though everyone knows that you are, and always will be, *balanda*.

PG   Yolŋu and *balanda*. Together, but not mixed up.

EG   Why do we do this work? Because the anthropologist wants us to work with her. The Yolŋu life stays in that one position and anthropologists come and ask, 'Can you work with me?' So Jennifer asked *mori* and *ŋändi*, our mum and dad, 'Can you work with me?' And she found the truth with *mori*, our dad. And she found it with our mum, who worked with us too, before she passed away.

PG   We call ourselves Miyarrka Media. Miyarrka is the name we call this region that includes Gapuwiyak and the outstations around here. We chose that name so that it could include all the clans who live in this community.

      I've been doing this kind of work my whole life, first as a dancer and then an actor. After that I toured around managing a group called the Yalakun Dancers. All over the world. Paris, Germany, America. Asia too. So in this *yuṯa* anthropology, this new anthropology, we want to make it so that anyone, even people in the States or China, can understand our lives by reading the book. With this *djorra'*.

                                    .

JD   Collaborating with Yolŋu means working with the irregular rhythms of lives shaped by stress of many kinds: poverty, welfare dependency, ill health, premature deaths, constantly shifting assimilationist policies and other forms of bureaucratically driven disempowerment and loss— all this strips meaning and purpose from the day-to-day. It is not just death that is relentless, it is the way that various accretions of loss, fear and disappointment shear away life itself. People are living very different lives to their fathers and grandfathers in over-crowded concrete houses, in communities starting to sprawl beyond the size that once made them comfortably intimate. The urge to find a means to relax is strong, whether through marijuana, or kava, or card games, or the lulling routines of bubble-shooting games played on the phone. Sometimes, when things just get too much or perhaps disappoint too often, the best-laid plans (and the people who make them) go awry. Often in extreme ways.

As effects accumulate, the rhythms of life become erratic. Sorrow and frustration take an enormous toll. And yet—and this is harder to talk about without sounding naïve, especially in the face of public discourses that consistently figure remote Aboriginal communities in terms of a back-sliding metrics of disadvantage—there is also a robustness to life in Arnhem Land that I find extremely compelling. People shape their days with a certain resilient vitality that is generous, funny and often wickedly clever.

Part of what I love about these creations is the way that they disrupt my, at times, overwrought tendency to figure their days as either sorrowful *or* vital, frustrated *or* happy, impoverished *or* funny. What I value most about these photographs is the ways that they allow strangers to apprehend something about Yolŋu life as it is made, and remade, framed as neither traditional culture nor assimilation. In the process, a quiet politics of affirmation is played out.

·

EG Jennifer's Yolŋu name is Bununuk. That's the name her *märi* gave her when we adopted her. She understands our life, but not everything. She still gets confused sometimes. So we help her and she helps us. We're a team, working together with *waŋgany muḻkurr, waŋgany ŋayaŋu.* One heart, one mind. That's what you have to do to get things done. Otherwise you are alone and nothing happens.

JD The word for maternal grandmother is *märi*, and this is perhaps the most important ritual relationship that Yolŋu have. If the calf is the part of the body assigned to one's brothers and sisters, your belly signifies your mother, your *märi* is your backbone, because the *märi* carries her grandchildren on her back.

JD   Despite my best efforts, I often make mistakes in my work as an anthropologist. These can be at the level of language and its transcription, or how I piece together a story out of the bits and pieces that people have given me over the years. Sometimes, I only recognise my mistakes in retrospect, once I've learned more. Unfortunately, Yolŋu are used to *balanda* getting things muddled. Though it must be extremely frustrating, I sometimes think that they find it a reassuring marker of the depth and complexity of what they hold dear.

Members of Miyarrka Media have known me long enough to know my limitations—linguistic, intellectual, emotional. I know theirs too. These understandings texture our relationship, and our anthropology. I work with people who implicitly understand that my perspective, no matter how soft-chested, will always necessarily be partial and positioned.

None of us are quite sure about how our *yuṯa* anthropology will be received by readers with whom we will likely never share the intimacies and struggles of daily life side-by-side, face-to-face and 'in the flesh'.

•

JD   *Together, but not mixed up.* This statement indicates more than the potential of our shared anthropology. As we will see in the chapters to follow, it is a statement about how Yolŋu approach the possibilities of being Yolŋu, Australians and participants in a global digital culture. As the phone brings new proximities, new relationships must necessarily be forged. The global did not pre-exist, it must be made.

Anna Tsing, thinking about the global from a very different vantage point, writes beautifully about collectives and assemblages. 'Assemblages... are open-ended gatherings. They allow us to ask about communal effects without assuming them. They show us potential histories in the making... Thinking through assemblages urges us to ask: How do gatherings sometimes become part of 'happenings,' that is, greater than the sum of their parts?'

•

ŊURRUWUTTHUN, EYE OF THE EAGLE
tKayleen Djingadjingawuy Waṉambi, 2017

GROWING UP THE SAME
Renelle Barraḏakanbuy Wunuŋmurra, 2013

Dubudubu is the name of this eagle. It's the name of this Ŋurruwutthun boy too. He has eyes like an eagle. See? Sharp eyes. Here they are in the sky together, high up where they can see anything, even small things, moving on the ground.

This boy follows the Eagles football team. He's the best player in his own team too. See the medals round his neck? They're from school sports.

This little boy recently started boarding school, because he's smart, smart, smart. The bird represents his *muḻkurr* [mind, head]. And he got a certificate with the eagle on it, because it represents the way he sees things from a long way away. He's smart.

KAYLEEN DJINGADJINGAWUY

This picture is about my youngest sister and her cousin-sister, Relda Malaguya Wunuŋmurra, growing up the same.

MEREDITH BALANYDJARRK

SHARK BOYS
Simeon Rigamawuy Wunuŋmurra, 2014

BÄRU
Kayleen Djingadjingawuy Waṉambi, 2015

These two Dätiwuy clan brothers call themselves shark boys. That's their identity and song. They know how to dance this and can be fierce and angry like the shark when he's speared, or when he smells blood and starts turning and thrashing in the water.

There's a special name for that splashing, shining and bubbling water the shark makes when it rises up. We call it *djarraran bunmirr*.

At the moment, these boys each live with a different grandmother in different communities. But here they are together again.

WARREN BALPATJI

This man, Michael Yawundjur Nungguldurpuy, is named after the crocodile. When you look at this photo through culture you see his special fire glowing in the mouth of the crocodile. You can see the strength of that man too.

That *bäru* [crocodile] from Baykurrtji gave the fire to other Yirritja clans. He flicked his hands and the sparks we called *nilŋnilŋ'* spread the flame to every place. There are only three people left from the Baykurrtji Mardarrpa clan. He sometimes feels very alone.

KAYLEEN DJINGADJINGAWUY

FOOTY STARS
Renelle Barradakanbuy Wunuŋmurra, 2013

SMM_JBW
Rowena Laypu Wunuŋmurra, 2008

The boys are surrounded by the colours of their homeland. Gordon's is blue for Luŋgutja, the island near Yalakun. Shadrick's is red, the colour from the Dhaḻwaŋu clan homeland of Gurrumuru. The stars are the Yirritja evening star, Djulpan.

KAYLEEN DJINGADJINGAWUY

Marrawaka'mirr's daughter Laypu named this file SMM_JBW before she sent it through to me in Cairns. Marrawaka'mirr and I are painted up with ochre to dance at the funeral in Gapuwiyak of my sister's son, who was murdered on the quiet suburban streets of Nhulunbuy.

The initials JBW stand for my Yolŋu name, Jennifer Bununuk Wunuŋmurra.

JENNIFER DEGER

EG   It's interesting to show our culture. To share us. They'll give us and we'll give them... What do *balanda* give us?... Wait, wait... respect, *ŋayaŋu*, *dharaŋan*, recognition. We don't want to hurt each other's feelings. We have to respect *balanda* and they will respect us. Because they want us to learn and we want them to learn with us. What Yolŋu life is really. It's a way of encouraging us.

PG   Everybody loves these *bitja* and all these new colours. So now in this book we are doing something new again. We have collected these *bitja* from our close family and then used the computer to make *bitja* with even more pattern and meaning. In this way, we can show how these *bitja* spread out to connect all Yolŋu families.

       In this book we are remixing the *bitja* to make new patterns. This brings more energy, more colour, more deep meanings and deeper richness of feeling, using new technologies that give us new ways to show the patterns and stories that make us who we are and where we belong and how we connect, whether we are walking around with a spear or with a phone.

JD   Given my Yolŋu colleagues' appreciation of the ways that telling stories and showing images are deeply social and political acts, they are acutely concerned not only about undue revelation of sacred sites, sights and stories, but about the potential to shame individuals and families, and so contribute to a fracturing of relationships rather than a unification. Their emphasis on performativity, aesthetics and social politics helped me to recognise the potential of this book in terms quite different to the social science I have been trained to produce.

       As the person responsible for the way the text came together for a *balanda* audience, my task lay in finding a means to allow for our different perspectives, ambitions and understandings to become (and remain) legible, even as we claimed a unifying purpose. I needed this to be a shared anthropology that made room for sometimes being at cross-purposes and misunderstanding one another. It was not enough to demonstrate the epistemological push-and-pull inherent to our work; my responsibility lay in finding a way for our voices to work together and so to enact the potential of becoming *waŋgany* that motivates us. After many months of false starts, I finally began to understand that my role was not simply to write, but to be a curator, a cut-and-paste text-maker involved an ethical-aesthetic art of assemblage.

JD   Balpatji adopted our designer, Santiago Carrasquilla, on the rooftop of his apartment in Brooklyn after we'd worked together on an exhibition installation. He gave him a Gurruwiwi name that means rainbow and the kin relation of *gäthu* [son]. Santiago had come up with the idea for the large collaged patterns that we displayed on large plywood boards at the American Museum of Natural History. They had worked so well as analogues for bark paintings that we decided to elaborate them further for this book.

PG   That Djäri is too clever with his computer. If you look at these new patterns he made and squint your eyes a little, they look like *gamunuŋgu*, like the ancestral designs that Yolŋu make. Just like those bark paintings that some Yolŋu sell in art galleries. Or give to museums. This way of showing the *bitja* brings more meaning, and deeper feelings. It's new and it's really *manymak*, really good and beautiful. And Yolŋu will love them.

JD   Gurrumuruwuy's *colour, pattern, lively* directive has meant making a commitment to work with a publisher who could enable us to publish in colour. To publish these images in black and white would have been to brutally disavow the very processes of enlivenment that we champion—and the materialisation of relationships that the colours themselves enact.

Given their original source, none of the images in this book are within the usual 300dpi range of acceptability for printing. That posed a significant challenge for the design, which we attempted to solve through the use of collage and gridded repetition to create a new kind of multi-image portrait style. Occasionally, though, we wanted to feature a large single image. Santiago became concerned that we were pushing the tiny images beyond their capacity to hold their own. For instance, the file size of the 'Shark Boys' image was technically way too small for the double-page spread we ended up giving it. Santiago's impulse to solve this dilemma was to work the image further through additional processes of scanning and digital effects. While the resulting image appeared more deliberately pixelated, it felt profoundly removed from the original. With the rest of the team more interested in the image than the 'non-professional' standard, Santiago acquiesced but asked that I acknowledge his misgivings about the blurry reproduction of that image and the large Elvis spread at the end of the book.

We spent quite some time on the cover design, creating a number of options to eventually settle on this version as the best way convey the book's content, themes and aesthetic intent. Initially, after feedback from a couple of colleagues, I had been concerned that the gridded arrangement of phones might be taken as yet another iteration of anthropology's long-standing and much-critiqued tendency towards collection, categorisation and display. These worries were allayed in discussions with Gurrumuruwuy and others who reminded me that this book refracts a visual economy with its own sophisticated sense of pattern, arrangement and allure—and its own located politics of strategically authorised revelation. For Gurrumuruwuy the priority was to come up with a cover that would attract potential readers. He approved of this cover because of the energy it exudes and range of relationships it invokes, seeing it as an apt 'background' for the deeper understandings to be disclosed within. For me, the decision to create a layout in which the phones extend beyond the confines of the page emphasises the phones as constituting their own grid of pattern (rather than as an array of collected objects), while gesturing also to the outward reach of connection enabled by the technology itself.

.

EG   Why do we do this work? Because *balanda* are interested in knowing about us. Through this anthropology we'll teach them what is Yolŋu life. Because anthropologists are teachers for *balanda*. If *balanda* don't know about our lives, they might go anywhere, ceremony or business side. So we are working to teach *balanda*—not just Bununuk, but all *balanda*—so that when they get to our community they already know and don't walk around everywhere, going where they are not allowed and maybe bumping into men's ceremonies.

PG   We want to show how wide and how deep Yolŋu can see... Maybe that way you can see something new too. Because when you look through your phone with Google or YouTube or any of those *bitja* and video and games, you can see that we are all together in a global world.

.

JD   In keeping with the spirit of remix and recombination that drives us, some texts that appear have been published elsewhere in different configurations. Similarly, the words have been assembled from various sources, including audio and video recordings.

With encouragement from Gurrumuruwuy, I took ideas and phrases from one source and added them to others. Listening to me read the resulting texts—sometimes over the phone and sometimes when we met in person—he endorsed this process. 'You patch it together and it becomes reality. It sounds strong. Brings more. Stronger.' At times he would add bits, or change the wording of his own statements. He would point out where I had got things wrong and we would find ways to fix the error. He understood that there are long sections written from my perspective as anthropological mediator, sometimes using dense and unfamiliar language as well as references. In keeping with the Yolŋu cultural logic of 'seeing for oneself' and 'speaking from one's own perspective and level of authority', it was agreed at the outset that we would all contribute to this book from our various points of view, as long as we did not say or show anything that might upset or shame relatives.

As we share this media—originally made for circulation amongst family members and never intended for display—we have tried to respect the personal and layered narratives they contain, providing detail enough so that the depths of the kinship they promote might begin to show themselves to strangers while staying within the realm of 'outside' knowledge. At the same time, we have tried to do justice to generations experimenting with ways to learn, connect and thrive, as they inhabit worlds of sensuous force and inside meanings, worlds that far exceed the registers of what the eye can see, the camera can capture, or, indeed, what this anthropologist will ever know.

•

PG   *Walŋa* is the Yolŋu word for alive. We are making an energetic *djorra'*. Not dry or boring! But powerful and alive, what we call *ganydjarrmirr.*

What is it to be human
with a mobile in hand?
How do these devices
change the ways we see?
What we look at? How
we care? What kinds
of intimacies are being
nurtured? What forms
of attentiveness tickled
to the fore?

JENNIFER DEGER

When the young people make those pictures on their phones what they are doing is making those photographs *waŋa* [talk, speak, ask for]. Yolŋu can hear that call. We can feel it.

PAUL GURRUMURUWUY

RED FLAG BOY
Simeon Rigamawuy Wunuŋmurra, 2009

Simeon used his phone to turn Wayne Guywuru into a movie star. See all the people sitting in the audience looking up at him? Guywuru is a Dhaḻwaŋu boy, he dances the red flag like his brothers and his fathers. That red flag has deep meanings for us. That's where his power comes from. See the heat in the letters? That shows his connection to that Dhaḻwaŋu place called Gurrumuru.

MEREDITH BALANYDJARRK

Guywuru is a big boy now. He's in Alice Springs doing a rehab program, getting away from *waymi* [grass] and *bitrul* [petrol]. His *momu* just came back from taking him down there. She still loves that Red Flag Boy *bitja*.

ENID GURUŊULMIWUY

Red Flag Boy is gone now. He passed away.

PAUL GURRMURUWUY

MÄRI IS OUR BACKBONE
Kayleen Djingadjingawuy Waṉambi, 2015

We took this photo at the opening of *Gapuwiyak Calling* exhibition in Cairns. The *bitja* shows Garkman, the green frog, who is the *märi* for all of us. *Märi* is the backbone for *gutharra*. Because *märi* carried our mum. Without *märi* you can't see the world.

Märi is the boss for everything and through the *maḏayin* [men's business] *märi* is boss for *gutharra*. Or,

the *gutharra* will control the *märi*. *Märi* will give permission to *gutharra* and then they will handle all the ceremonial work. So the *märi* is strictly controlling and watching over everything. For all Yolŋu.

MEREDITH BALANYDJARRK

The phone helps young people upgrade their connections. Most people are doing this. Even if you don't know your *gamuɲgu*, you can see it.

JAMES GANAMBARR

GUMATJ FIRE
Jessica Ganambarr, 2014

The Gumatj clan sing that special fire [*gurtha*]. Lots of different clans have fire, but Gumatj people have this one, with their different *gakal* [style] and different meanings. They put themselves in the *gurtha* because they belong to that *gurtha* and their grandfather. Not only *gurtha*, but *bäru* [crocodile] and *maranydjalk* [stingray]. It tells straight away that they are Gumatj.

See the ways the *gurtha* shines in their faces? It looks like they're facing their father. And that's got meaning. The faces shining, reflecting the fire. It's their identity and their power.

ENID GURUŊULMIWUY

PARTICIPATORY POIESIS

PART II

PARTICIPATORY POIESIS

PARTICIPATORY POIESIS

JD We are not the first to write about the rapid and enthusiastic uptake of mobile phone technologies in remote Aboriginal communities. A number of researchers have described the new kinds of social tensions arising as a result of being able to communicate person-to-person over long distances, in ways that cannot be locally monitored, much less contained.

In Arnhem Land, as elsewhere, the mobile phone has become something of a lightning rod for morally charged discussions about the problems of our times, being widely recognised as a source of social disruption and intergenerational tension. My Yolŋu friends describe their children becoming 'addicted' to their phones, rendered mute and unresponsive to what is going on around them as they play games, tease, flirt and fight. In a place where so many interactions happen in the full light of public scrutiny, the phone offers an alternative conduit for social relations—a means, for instance, for conducting improper relationships beyond the shaming gaze of kin. The phone is also blamed for encouraging anonymous intimidation and bullying, not to mention Internet banking abuse, social security fraud and sexualised self-display.

I heard recently of a young Yolŋu man jailed for attacking his estranged girlfriend with a mobile phone. This seemed such a poignant poetics, such a Yolŋu way of expressing the dynamics of desire and frustration, connection and disconnection, acknowledgement and refusal that the phone materialises: the phone as a weapon; the phone as a new means of cruelty and violence; the phone as new a source of vulnerability.

Yet these are not the stories my Yolŋu collaborators wish to tell in *Phone & Spear*. The other members of Miyarrka Media have no interest in casting their lives in the language of crisis and social decay that inflects so many discussions about Aboriginal communities. Neither is the book concerned to point out, or analyse, the forms of structural violence and inequity that give rise to the so-called 'gap' between Aboriginal people and the rest of Australian society: a chasm of disadvantage manifest in the shaming national statistics of Indigenous life expectancy, education outcomes, employment and rates of incarceration.

On the pages of *Phone & Spear* you will find no accusation, no demand, no call for pity, nor institutionalised action. Although people routinely complain about exhaustion, poverty, expressing ongoing frustration at not being able to access enough resources to keep their cars on the road, or food in the fridge, my co-authors are not compelled to critically engage these aspects of their life circumstances. Nor to frame our work as a form of anticolonial struggle.

Instead, as part of a reflexive and explicitly interculturally orientated project of sharing Yolŋu life, Miyarrka Media choose to emphasise the value of 'using the phone in a good way': to show that it is possible to 'put the phone into *rom*', as Guruŋulmiwuy says.

At a time when it is all too easy for outsiders to see only fracture and enervation, the phone-made images we share attest to the astonishingly imaginative dexterity and deep sincerity with which Yolŋu bring seemingly disparate things together to make them one, or *waŋgany*, by activating ancestrally patterned constellations of relationship and story. With calculated audacity this art generates a moral charge that goes beyond familiar discussions about the effects of mobile phones in *balanda* life. What this phone-made media shows, in other words, is that 'good' need not mean boring, or predictable. Media scholars might refer to this as the 'ancestral affordances' of the mobile phone.

We consider that this work makes visible something that, from a Yolŋu perspective, really matters: it is not only about the dynamics of digital life, but about the values and practices that sustain a relational life more generally.

■

JD Yolŋu routinely describe themselves as living in two worlds: Yolŋu and *balanda*. This is how Gurrumuruwuy characterises the difference: 'Yolŋu have their life already there, *balanda* have to chase their life through the *djäma*, through their work and careers.'

I would add that while the Yolŋu world is already there—encompassing, patterned and full of sacred depth, meaning and authority—it must nonetheless be reproduced, made and remade with fulsome zest and due respect. Each ceremony, each car ride, each television set lugged from house to house, gives shape to life patterned by kinship. Moment by moment the world is made over as a synaesthetic field of colour, pattern, story and relationship. Therein lies the *djäma* of the Yolŋu world.

However, Yolŋu must constantly manage their lives in what seems to me to be a brutalising push-and-pull between these two worlds with such different foundational structures and values.

Almost invariably, they chose the Yolŋu world when it comes to being forced to make a decision between, for instance, family and employment obligations; or when weighing up the validity of the medical facts delivered by coroner investigating an unexpected death against the carefully accrued evidence gleaned from a close, retrospective examination of past events (sometimes referred to as *CSI, Yolŋu-style*), evidence suggesting the real cause of death is *galka djäma* [sorcery]. Nonetheless, my Yolŋu friends do not disavow the *balanda* world as an integral part of their lives. Guruŋulmiwuy—who currently lives in Darwin with her husband Balpatji, working part-time for an Indigenous catering company, and who animatedly tells me that she now knows how to lay a table with knives, forks and champagne glasses—is immensely pragmatic in this respect, explaining, 'We need to have a foot in both worlds. Otherwise we will lose our balance. Otherwise, we will fall over.'

·

JD   Even as we have selectively crafted a book around ancestrally ordered, cut-and-paste patterns—and taking a distinctive pleasure declaring them to be *gamunuŋgu* in a new guise—we have not sought to deny, or otherwise exclude, the fracturing and dissolution that equally characterises contemporary Yolŋu life. While it enables new forms of sensuously mediated kinship, the mobile also makes for new pressures that have to be managed—and, indeed, gives new material form, and satellite-assisted projective reach, to the fractious forces shaping the contemporary Yolŋu world. And thus the accretions and disjuncture and loss that now determine so much of everyday life sit close to the surface in the stories we tell and the images we show.

Yet, as I have indicated, my Yolŋu colleagues have no interest in rendering their lives in terms of social crisis. What matters to them—and what they, from the outset, have been adamant that this book should affirm—is how such phone-made media can evidence a kind of counter-force of structuring pattern and story, even as they quietly acknowledge fears about the 'collapse of *rom*' or the future as already 'wrecked'.

The point of the book, then, is performative of the relational dynamics of Yolŋu life, not only as it extends to the readers of this book. Even as the images, stories and ringtones that we share in the book acknowledge layers of loss, death and intergenerational friction, they mediate forms of connectedness *Yolŋu-style*, with the effect of energising and affirming a social network of moral force and consequence with roots in the land and the sea.

Rapidly evolving digital technologies further complicate, and would seem to challenge, any notion of truly separate worlds because of the fact that devices, and the multitude of media apps that can be download onto them at minimal cost, provide the means for new modes of participatory world-making. Indeed, the free photo collage apps and websites that Yolŋu regularly access explicitly promote themselves in a language of co-creativity, sharing and empowerment that celebrates a world no longer necessarily structured by geographic, or cultural, separation.

Mark C. Taylor writes in less-than-euphoric terms when he laments the disappearance of place 'as a result of an unprecedented accelerating intersection of globalization, virtualization, and cellularization'. Yet the co-creative dynamics of the mobile media we share focus on place-based belonging; they demonstrate how sensuous relationships with the land, the sea, the spirits of the ancestors, and indeed the recently deceased, can be evoked, mediated and affirmed by using mobile phones. In the chapters that follow we will show how Yolŋu use their phones in ways that both challenge and extend presumptions about what it means to creatively participate in the call-and-response of digitally mediated relationships.

In addition, we will see how these phones enable the work of what members of Miyarrka Media describe as *yuṯa rom*. As Yolŋu play with form and content through the rudimentary media functions of their handsets, the old and the new are made co-constitutive. The new renews the old, while the old inheres inside the new, as a new generation demonstrates a dextrous grasp of a here-and-now made confidently resonant across Yolŋu configurations of time and space.

·

JD   In the chapters that follow we will highlight the phone-made acts of participatory poiesis, as *yuṯa*-generation Yolŋu use Google and YouTube to bring forth, make visible, enliven and affirm a Yolŋu world open to moving ever closer into relationship with *balanda*, while remaining resolutely distinct and separate.

Like the media that inspires it, this section of the book deliberately pulls together selected stories and ideas to demonstrate the possibility of rendering the world in various configurations of *waŋgany*-ness, so enacting one more moment in a long and ongoing Yolŋu history of making and remaking a world of relational constellations through creative action, associative thinking, situated politics and kin-based social structures. The forms of co-creativity that concern us here exceed the way it is usually discussed by media scholars concerned to highlight, and critically analyse, the participatory processes and innovations made possible by new conjunctions of technologies, organisations and participants. For this is a form of technologically mediated collaboration that explicitly extends beyond human networks and digital forms. It understands collaboration as the manifestation of a relational ethos in which one participates with the self-revealing forces of a patterned world.

CALL & RESPONSE

JD There are days when I want to hurl my phone into the sea. Most nights I sleep with it pressed under my pillow.

buzz, shudder, grasp
text, image, video, voice
send, delete, ignore, reject, reply, like, share
call & response
call & response
call & response

Somehow it's the act of not answering that requires the most energy.

Often when my phone rings and the call is from Arnhem Land, I wonder if I'm really up to the demands of this work. Quite often—and I've had to practise this, schooled by my Yolŋu kin themselves—I don't pick up. Only after five or six attempts (I find such insistence particularly Yolŋu) does the phone finally stop its wilful shudder.

Gurrumuruwuy laughed when I read these lines to him. He suggested I buy a new SIM card. 'You make it too easy. Anyone can find you.' I do a quick tally of the phone numbers I've had for him over the years. More than fifteen, I reckon, whereas I've had the same number the whole time.

■

JD Nothing materialises the push-and-pull of contemporary life like mobile phones. It is the aesthetic medium of our time—a device through which sound, images and touch give shape and force to worlds of sensation and meaning assembled on the move.

Of course, I had no sense of this when I bought my first mobile in 2005, the same year mobile phone connection finally came to Arnhem Land. I just wanted to talk with people. For many months before the Telstra network was switched on in this remote corner of northern Australia, my Yolŋu friends and family looked forward to a new technology that would allow us all to keep in more regular contact. Previously, if I needed to get hold of them I had to call one of three public phone boxes in the community and ask whoever happened to answer to search out the person I was ringing. This system worked better than one might think.

Back then I had no inkling of how much these new devices were to contribute to the deepening (and, at times, the testing) of my relationships with Yolŋu. Nor did I anticipate the degree to which my practice-based research methods would come to depend on media made and distributed via mobile phones.

A year later, I took my first trip with my first mobile. Within hours of my arrival at the home of my closest Yolŋu kin, the Nokia was given a customised ringtone. Originally recorded on a reel-to-reel in 1996 by a Canadian ethnomusicologist, this ringtone, and the song series it comes from, had been copied and repatriated to Gapuwiyak on CD more times than I can remember. In a time before memory cards and USB sticks, they used their phones to record whatever they wanted straight from the stereo speaker. No one ever asked me for the CD version again.

The choice of track, selected by them and sung by their fathers—my late Yolŋu brother and video collaborator Bäŋgana Wunuŋmurra and his brother Bruce Burrimbirr—could not have been more deliberate. This song is about the great Yirritja moiety Lightning Snake, Gatj, who calls to other clans by spitting lightning into the sky. At the beginning of the wet season, when Gatj tastes the first flush of fresh waters surging through the brackish swamps, he rears high above the Dhaḻwaŋu clan saltwater country of Garraparra to signal to other snakes, in other Yirritja homelands. They, in turn, reciprocate with their own lightning, thereby affirming the connections between the different clans.

Bäŋgana's daughters chose that track to perform our enduring connection in very Yolŋu terms: not only through the poetics of positioning me as a Dhaḻwaŋu person being called, but by bringing to the fore the surge of powerful feelings created by shared attachment and loss.

And so my mobile no longer simply rang—it called.

•

JD Every time I heard that ringtone (and we soon worked out how to play the song only when my Yolŋu family called), it evoked in me a complex mix of feelings and memories, anticipation and obligation. By locating me within a very specific network of relationship, it made me more receptive to the news, the stories and the frequent demands. About two years

Gu gu
Ŋarra nhuŋgu Yilparawuy
barkbarkkun
Yä nhuŋgu ŋänha'ŋanharaw
Yä man'tjarr
Wukundurr Gänaŋur gälam marrtji
Ah miwatj Baruŋganŋur wukundurr
Dhä-nherran marrtji makala
Wurrunymulkanharaw
Dhamburrdhamburrwuŋ
Man'tjarr yiwaŋa galirrwara
wukundurr
Yä ŋäthil dhakunmaraŋ Yakutjawuyŋu
Dhuŋungaḻ Meŋurryu
Yä ŋäthil dhakunmaraŋ Yakutjawuyŋu
Baraltjawuyŋu

(humming)
Yämalwaŋa mundumundu
wu wu gatj gatj

Gänaŋur gälam marrtji
Miwatj Baruŋganŋur
Wumitjitji
Dhä-nherran marrtji makaḻa
Wurrunymulkanhawuy

Yä ŋäthil dhakunmaraŋ Yakutjawuyŋu
Dhuŋungaḻwuyŋu
Yä ŋäthil dhakunmaraŋ Yakutjawuyŋu
Baraltjawuyŋu

Dhalalyun wukuyun
Mundumundu mundu
gapu-waykarraŋmirri

wu wu gatj gatj

(humming)
wu wu gatj gatj

Yä
First float of Manjarr leaf to of
Yakutja Dhuŋungaḻ
Meŋurryu
Yä
First float of Yakutja of Baraltja

Rainbow Serpent Rainbow Serpent
Yä yä wu wu gatj gatj

From Gana floating floating
Different from Baruŋgan
Leaves floating floating leaves
floated

Yä first float of Yakutja of Dhuŋungaḻ
Yä first float of Yakutja of Baraltja

Floating spitting out lightning
Rainbow Serpent Rainbow Serpent
with clear water

later, when the 3G network and camera phones finally became available in Gapuwiyak and neighbouring communities, I received an image. My *gäthu* instructed me to make it my wallpaper.

The *bitja* features Bäŋgana looking outwards and smiling. It's a photograph of a photograph; a photograph of the photograph on his headstone. This image has been framed using a preloaded generic template: a coconut-tree-lined beach sunset scene. Additional flecks of light have been added.

EG   At the very beginning of that recording our brother Bruce talks into the tape to say that this is for the new generation to come. Those two brothers who made that recording gave their voices and images for the new generation to come. They all do it when they record themselves. They make recordings for the kids who don't know and they always say, *this is for family when I die.*

·

JD   Bäŋgana's widow, Susan Marrawaka'mirr, texts me only when she has no credit. Often, she wants me to deposit thirty-five dollars in her bank account for a pack of cigarettes. But sometimes when I call back she'll put the phone on speaker and I'll hear the voice of a man quietly singing to the beat of his lighter (in lieu of clapsticks) striking the floor. This is how families now deliver the news of a death to those of us who aren't there in person to hear the formal ceremonial announcement.

Late one afternoon in 1995, I watched while Bäŋgana carried a hefty, portable CD-cassette player to the public phone box about 100 metres from his house. Balancing it on the edge of the little stainless-steel shelf, he dialled a neighbouring community and waited until the person he was calling, the wife of a man who had died in a car crash, came to the phone. The Darwin newspapers had reported the cause of death as drunken misadventure, but most Yolŋu attributed it to the work of *galka*. After some time the woman came on the line and Bäŋgana apologised for being unable to attend the funeral. He then held the receiver to the cassette player's speaker as he played the dead man's favourite song. When it finished, he wound it back to the beginning and they listened again.

Yolŋu call this deliberate triggering of sentiment through sensory memory *warwuyun*. This verb often gets glossed as 'worry' when people talk about it in English, but it's a translation that's hardly adequate.

•

JD   In 2014, we interviewed Bäŋana's second-born daughter, Yawulwuy, for the Miyarrka Media film *Ringtone*. Her youngest sister dialled the number to trigger the ringtone. She let the music play then answered the phone, snapping it closed before talking straight into the lens of the camera: 'This is my father singing on my ringtone. I chose this one because I miss him. He's been dead now for twelve years. When it comes on I'm reminded of him,' she said.

Her sister, Lay'pu, told a similar story, but from a different perspective. 'This song is from my *waku* [children's clan]. It also reminds me of my mother because it's her *märi*'s clan song. My two children and my husband... this clan song makes me think of them. It's also my father's *momu*'s [father's mother's] song. So with this song I think about them all. Right now I'm thinking and worrying about them all'.

•

JD   What is it to be human with a mobile in hand? How do these devices change the ways we see? What we look at? How we care? As social media enables us to maintain our relationships through heart-shaped icons and the click of an onward share button—giddy participants in new economies of affect and image—what is being left unsaid, unseen, unnoticed or, even, deliberately disregarded? What kinds of intimacies are being nurtured? What forms of attentiveness tickled to the fore?

When I put these questions to Gurrumuruwuy, he answered with quick assurance: 'It depends how you see it. It depends how you use your phone.'

•

PG   One word we use for mobile phones is *rirrakay*. That means like sound or voice. Because that phone is always calling you; making sounds, grabbing your attention, pulling you close. Yolŋu have many words for mobile phones. Another one is *waya*. *Waya* is the electric cord that you plug into the wall so that your fridge or your television comes on. Or your computer. The phone is *waya* too because you make that connection straight away, but with people far away. Another word we can use is *raki'*. That means like a vine, or a string, or a cable. We call the phone *raki'* because you can easily contact someone far away through the *raki'*.

.

PG   *Manymak.* So far, so good. With this picture, with what I've just told you, you can see the outside part of what I'm talking about. But if you look underneath, if you look deeper in a Yolŋu way, then you can see that we are talking about something more than the connections that Telstra can give you. *Raki'* means that the phone can be the connection to your *wäŋa* [land], your *gurruṯu* [family], your culture, your *rom*.

We use *raki'* in ceremonies. It shows deep connections through *gurruṯu*; that means family, what anthropologists call kinship. That's how the old people see it. That's what they mean when they talk about the phone as *raki'*. But young people can get confused by that. So if I tell a young person, 'Bring me my *raki''*, they might bring back a fishing line. Because they don't see the phone as *raki'*. They're floating on the top of the vine, they're not rooted to the soil and where it goes and what it means.

So these days, you hear people complaining that there's too many *raki'* around. People can talk in all directions, to their boyfriend, their boss, to anyone. That means that your *raki'* might be pulling you away from *rom*. Because through the phone you can make all kinds of connections, nobody knows what you're really up to. You can be talking this way and that way. Anyway, everyway. Before, people could look at a person and straight away they could see who they are and where they connect to. They could see their *rom*. Like when you see someone with a *gara* or *galpu*, a spear or a spear thrower, straight away you know it's an old man full of story, with *manikay*, *riŋgitj*, song and land and connection, everything all around him.

Nowadays these connections are going here and there, all over the place, through those *raki'*. Might be wrong-skin boyfriend, or girlfriend, might be this way or that way. Old people like me, we don't like this. But it's hard to control. Young people, they are nothing. Even with their phones, they're nothing.

WB   We are talking about spears now for this project because they are the fastest connection, they make connections with the land and the people. When those *mokuy* [ancestral beings] threw their spears they created the land, the sacred objects and designs, the songs and the languages. There are different beliefs and different stories that belong to different clans. Different people, different clans, different *bäpurru* have different ways of looking at their life and stories. Dhuwa people especially have stories about spears.

But we don't want to go off-track. We don't want to talk about other people's stories. Here when we talk about the spear, we are only talking about it from our own lives and knowledge, from the present day, a time when we have phones in our pockets and we only use the spear for ceremony, or hunting turtle and fish.

PG   There are three spears we can use. One is for fighting, one is for spearing fish and one is a harpoon for turtle.

.

PG   If you can't make it to a ceremony, like for example a circumcision or a funeral, you can make a video call. That way you can see the painting they're doing for those young boys, you can look at the coffin, you can hear the *manikay*, you can watch the *buŋgul* [dancing], see the gravesite and you can be with family, sending your feelings to be with them. Lots of times you see people walking around with their phone like that. Like I said before, phones are useful.

KD   When I talk about phones and spears, I'm thinking about my phone from my own *muḻkurr*, my own mind. From the perspective of my own *bäpurru*, my own clan. When I tell you my phone is like a spear, I'm talking about aim and goal. Like in the olden days they carried the *gara* for hunting animals, the spear was for food. But these days we use the phone for people to send us money for *ŋatha* [food], so we can go shopping.

We ring up, where's my money? Where's my food? We *ringem-up, ringem-up, ringem-up* until someone in our family can send us some money and we feed the kids and everyone.

PG   If you have a job, everyone has your phone number. And they ring, ring, ring.

DHÄWU GA MANIKAY
Simeon Rigamawuy Wunuŋmurra, 2015

COCONUT
Rowena Laypu Wunungmurra, 2008

That shark is telling stories, giving Deven knowledge, *rom*, and *manikay*.

MEREDITH BALANYDJARRK

In our work together Bäŋgana often referred to himself as a 'coconut', playfully inverting the insult 'black on the outside, white on the inside', to claim not only his exceptional skills in the *balanda* world, but at the same time to show his Dhaḻwaŋu relationship to Ḻuŋgutja, the island off the coast of Yalakun.

JENNIFER DEGER

Coconuts float from place to place, linking up places and people.

PAUL GURRUMURUWUY

We are talking about spears now for this project because they are the fastest connection, they make connections with the land and the people.

JAMES GANAMBARR

.

JD   At the beginning of this year I turned my phone off for three months, overwhelmed by the calls from Yolŋu in need of help with money, Internet banking, shopping, car repairs and paperwork for boarding school enrolments. When I did turn my phone on again, I received two calls within half-an-hour. Both from Yolŋu, people I am close to: one was looking for money for cigarettes, the other was in need of $570 to pay for her son's plane trip home. I transferred the money for cigarettes, made excuses to the mother in need and switched it off again for another month. To concentrate on the book, I told myself, irony duly noted. I was *hiding*, as Gurrumuruwuy puts it. No denying it. He does it too. The pressures on him are far greater. In fact, he's started to keep his phone turned off, switching it on only when he wants to make a call, or is waiting on one.

.

JD   In her book about the social effects of mobile phones in the United States, Sherry Turkle also talks about hiding, but in a different sense. She points to the ways that mobile phones enable individuals to 'hide from each other, even as we are constantly connected to each other'. Her argument is that while 'technology proposes itself as the architect of our intimacies', in fact, digital devices such as mobile phones erode proper human intimacy, producing new and profound forms of isolation and aloneness. She goes on to argue that as we become increasingly intimate with our machines, rather than with our friends and families, we lose touch with essential human experiences and values.

While I appreciate Turkle's argument, I have never heard Yolŋu express concern that machine-mediated relationships might become substitutes for real intimacy. Rather, the opposite is true: people worry that the phone enables too many intimacies and with that comes vulnerabilities of a different kind to those that preoccupy Turkle. For Yolŋu, phone-mediated connections can threaten the social structure because they happen outside of the scrutiny of a public gaze, enabling young people, especially, to have affairs with wrong-skin relations. They can threaten the physical integrity of individuals because the phone leaves them vulnerable to sorcerers, who call with silent messages that are transmitted through the ear, sent to lodge as a kind of time bomb within the person's body so that days later they will act on these embedded instructions, maybe killing someone, or hanging themselves—innocent of the action, captive to the violent volition of another.

•

JD   I remember talking to Marrawaka'mirr, my sister-in-law, about what it would be like when phones with cameras became available. She said she looked forward to being able to photograph *galka*, to scaring them away with the threat of being able to muster visible evidence not only of their existence, but their specific identity. I've yet to see a *galka* 'caught in the act'.

•

JD   The fact that people now use their phones for Internet banking and online welfare management opens up another source of pressure and vulnerability, along with the worry that younger, tech-savvy family members might help themselves to funds without permission.

So, for Yolŋu, the most pressing question is not what happens to society when people are constantly tethered to their phone and therefore always 'on', as Turkle puts it; rather, it is about managing the stresses and conflicts that arise from making oneself too available.

•

JD   Yolŋu change their numbers and, indeed, the phones themselves and the SIM cards for lots of reasons. Sometimes it's because their phone is broken, accidentally or otherwise, and so it's just more convenient to start afresh with the number that comes with the replacement handset. (Many Yolŋu do not realise that they can contact Telstra and arrange to keep their old number.) At other times, people change the SIM card because they feel exposed by the fact that so many people, including strangers, may access their number.

In the 1990s, the few Yolŋu who did have phones in their homes managed this simply by pulling the plug out of the wall socket for long stretches of time, or whenever it felt necessary.

EG   Unknown callers, they're not showing their number or identity... So people get worried. They think it might be *galka* calling. Someone trying to kill them through the phone. But sometimes it's just other Yolŋu trying to tease them, or scare them, making noises or whispering threats. Like when someone in a family dies, it might be someone will ring up from an unknown number and say, 'You'll be next.'

When this happens, people get scared. They might change their mobile phones but keep the same SIM card. Other times they swap SIM cards with other Yolŋu. So you call someone, but someone else picks up. They say hello, but it's another person. The owner of that SIM card changed it.

WB   It's like that. Yolŋu are always changing their mobile phones. And their SIM cards. Because they don't trust other Yolŋu with their numbers.

JD   Years ago, when I tried to call Bäŋgana's eldest daughter, Ŋumbagawuy, in Darwin after she'd given birth to her first child, she didn't answer. In fact, as she told me later with a shy laugh, because she didn't recognise my number my numerous attempts to make contact had completely freaked her out.

·

KD   Right now, Yolŋu are buying phones all the time. Quick, quick, *bäyim*, get those new-release models... young people especially. If you win at cards, straight away, off you go, buy a new phone.

EG   Some Yolŋu are really clever, changing their SIM card every month, or every week. Sometimes Yolŋu have multiple SIM cards, but just one ŋara-ka [carapace, shell or bone]. Maybe five or six SIM cards. Maybe they just have one SIM card with each phone and they change between phones. There's lots of different ways to do it. Yolŋu have lots of different ideas.

My little sister has four mobile phones. One is for playing games, one for music, one for Facebook or AirG and one for *hello hello*. She stays in her room and plays all day on her phone. She can go to the AirG or Facebook having a conversation with her friends. Technology gives too many ideas.

PG   The young people, they love it. Older people too. They still change their phone number if they're smart.

EG   Sometimes in a community when there's a lot of trouble and shouting.

Then they break it. Then straight away get a new one, with a new SIM card.

Sometimes we call Garrawara [another name for Gurrumuruwuy] and he just closes his phone and changes to another one.

KD   You know, for a long time Yolŋu people have been changing phones, like me. But this time my phone is the same one, because in my life I need to keep that same phone number, instead of switching to another number, so that my whole family in Milingimbi and other places—from the childcare and the clinic, all those organisations—they know my number. They can ring me straight, instead of trying other people's phones, this way and that. So they can talk direct to me.

EG   Sometimes I buy a new SIM card at the shop and I put the old one in the rubbish. Or I give it to someone else.

It might be people have one phone for their boyfriend or girlfriend and another one for their other family; one that they keep for talking to their kid at boarding school; and a secret one as back-up.

KD   When you carry your *gara*, if that *gara* breaks with a *yindipuy mäṉa*, on a really big shark, you can leave him there, get another one.

·

JD   In 2012, the wallpaper on Gurrumuruwuy's phone featured his late wife, Yangathu. I'd taken the shot while we were in Darwin planning an exhibition. Two weeks later, out of the blue, Yangathu was dead from melioidosis, a bacterial disease contracted through contact with soil.

For several years after she died, Gurrumuruwuy stayed in the long grass, living rough in Darwin, assuaging his sorrow and fury with too much grog and not enough food. His ringtone featured a song about a *mokuy* [spirit, ancestral figure] who cries as he searches for lost loved ones in the Dhaḻwaŋu homeland of Balambala. 'Are you alive? Or are you gone?' the *mokuy* calls to the land and the spirits that live there.

·

JG   When it comes to connecting with the *wäŋa*, the land and environment, the signal is always there. It's not like Telstra. You don't get disconnected.

.

JD   Working with Yolŋu has made me attuned to the power of resonance. Without it, our world seems staccato and slippery-thin, life's endings too brutally final, the grabby inertia of the day-to-day just plain exhausting. By making ideas, people, places and images resonate with each other, we call into being—and locate ourselves within—worlds of tremulous relationality. This is the stuff of kinship proper: worlds revealed as generative, patterned by cross-cuttings of similitude and difference, structured through an ethics of affinity.

.

PG   Through the phone you can see the *yindi* picture; the big picture, it tells you the story of the land, all the places, belonging to you. Even when you are sitting here you can feel *wata*, you feel the breeze because through that ringtone you can see your homeland. You feel that wind and your spirit will be drawn back to the land. To your mother's homeland, or your homeland. For example, with my phone, I hear my ringtone and it's like I'm worrying under the funeral shade still... it's like I'm at that ceremony and I'm worrying... it's growing in my mind and heart, the feelings... all through the phone.

.

JD   A dynamic of call and response creates worlds in quite particular ways. To set up this dynamic is to produce moments of enlivening; as one draws the other into openness and action, something new comes into the world, something that would not exist without the incitement of the other.

This mode of co-creation—*you do your part* then *I'll join in with mine*—affirms relationships structured by a certain formal separation (think the preacher and the choir, or Peter Frampton and his talking guitar, or if you know how, the *djirrikay* and the *yawirriny'* (the ritual leader and the boys who answer his call in ceremonies such as the revelatory rite recorded in our film *Manapanmirr, in Christmas Spirit*), and, in so doing, it makes a particular claim on life's participatory potential. Perhaps, in the process, it also asserts a kind of demand?

■

JD   For Gurrumuruwuy, it doesn't matter that he's never physically visited Balambala. He knows it from singing it, dancing it, imagining it—going there with his mind and heart. It's not at all unusual for Yolŋu to not have physically visited many of the key places in the songs they dance and sing to enact episodes and events that occurred in the travels of ancestral beings across the region.

I asked him what it's like when you go to somewhere that you have come to know in your mind and heart through the *manikay*.

'You look around and you think, so this is it,' he said.

A few months later, we're in Paris together for a film festival, all credit for international calls spent. It's late and I fall asleep to the sound of that same song playing through the tinny speakers of Gurrumuruwuy's phone. As he blows cigarette smoke out the window into the freezing French night, the song takes him home. 'It's just like being there,' he tells me in the morning. 'Just like sitting on the ground.'

■

PG   Everywhere you go people are using their phones to make connections to the land, even out to the sea; you see it with your mind using the songs on your phone. Dhuwa and Yirritja *mala*. You see the old people and you worry for them. You think about the old times, using these *yuṯa* technologies. Those old songs, like country-and-western love songs, like Elvis Presley or Charlie Pride. They make you remember when you were young.

JD   Could it be that the phone makes Yolŋu life possible in the city? Keeping people connected through song and story and *gurruṯu*, even if they are far away from their *wäŋa*? It might be the technology that changes everything about where people choose to live, letting people get training and jobs, while keeping connected to the *maḏayin*, land, and the old people through their phones? Can Yolŋu use this technology to live a new kind of life, that's still an old kind of life?

PG   Maybe. I don't know.

This ringtone is from my *märi*, Dhukuyuna from the Wagilak clan. I picked this song because it is sung by my number-two *märi*, called Larr. Larr has ancestral connections to my first *märi* clan at Mandi Raymaŋgirr.

When I hear this song I think of a close relative, someone I call *märi*, dancing as a spirit in her country. She's been drinking in the city and I dread a call telling me she's passed away. Whenever the phone rings, no matter who is calling, it's her voice I hear.

DAVID WÄPIT MUNUŊGURR

This is my clan's *guku* honey ringtone. Every time I hear it, I feel heartbreak. With this *guku* ringtone, I worry about my girlfriend so far away. I listen to this *guku* song and worry because we're apart. This is my clan *guku* ringtone. Sometimes I get sick from thinking about her too much. I get headaches from this ringtone.

CURTIS DHAMBALI WUNUŊMURRA

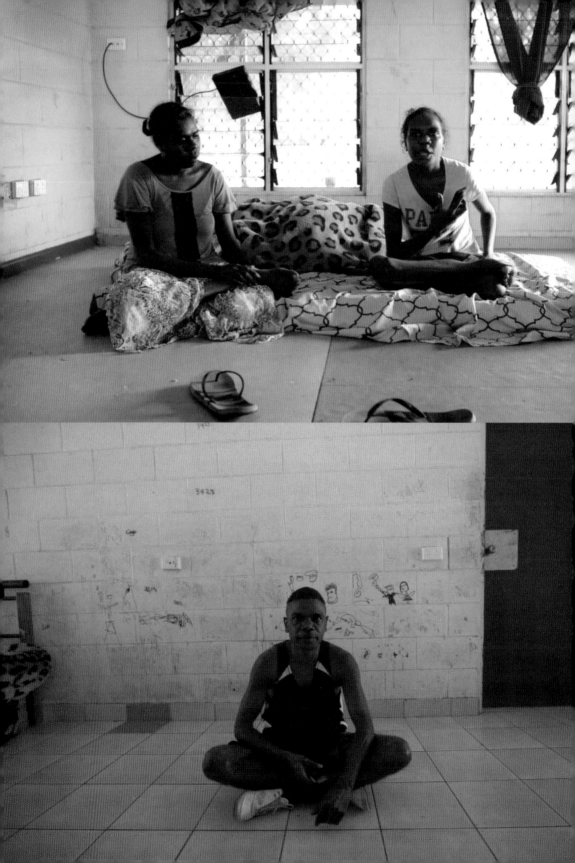

This ringtone is my favourite music for dancing in Darwin nightclubs. I dance with my friends at the disco, enjoying life and staying up until six in the morning with the *balanda*. We stay up to six o'clock in the morning, until the nightclub closes.

GEORGINA WARRITJA WUNUŊMURRA

I chose this ringtone [This Ain't Livin' by Tupac] so that I'll never be bored. This music makes me feel cool all the time. This is my favourite music. I love it. I never tire of it. I listen to it wherever I go.

MIKE YAMITJAWUY WUNUŊMURRA

I chose this *guku* honey song for my ringtone, because it's my ŋändi's [mother's] song and also my children's clan song. No matter where I go, when it rings I listen. Even in the city when I hear this I start to miss my family. I think and worry and my mind returns to that land at Raymaŋgirr and all my family. That's my mother country and all those people belong to that place.

My mother was a Marraŋu clan woman from Raymaŋgirr. This ringtone belongs to her clan, to my two uncles and my two mothers. That's why I chose that *guku* honey ringtone. It reminds me of fundamental family connections. When I'm away, I listen and I worry. I miss my grandson Bathulumi or I worry for my husband George, and for that homeland of Raymaŋgirr. I worry also about Ŋarritj, my other grandson, far away in hospital. That's why this song suits us all. We are all related through Raymaŋgirr.

That;s why this *guku* honey song sits in my heart, connecting me to all my family, everywhere.

JOYCE WALIKURR WUNUŊMURRA

My ringtone is Garkman, the green frog, and I really love it. When I'm falling asleep or out walking, I'm always listening to Garkman.

When others hear it, at the shop or wherever, they ask, 'What's this great frog ringtone?'

Garkman is my *märi* and this lady calls Garkman *waku* [son or daughter].

When I visit my family they say, 'Wow. That Garkman is such a lovely ringtone.' And I say, 'That's my *märi*, the green frog.'

LINDSAY LOPURRU WUNUŊMURRA

ALIVE!

KD   Yolŋu *biyarrmak* [funny, clowning around] videos started with the phones. The boys especially love to film themselves.

PG   Yolŋu have been doing funny dancing for a long time. They can dance like this in circumcision ceremonies, like when ladies dance like men and grab the *yidaki* [didgeridoo] for themselves. Those boys know there is something big coming up and we can take their mind away from this for a while. It is a way of mixing things up, to relax and have fun. Now we know how to use new technologies like phones and websites to gather new things together.

KD   We jump through the phone to find new ideas, styles and moves, and bring them back. Then we use our phones to film ourselves dancing from the music they collect. We can mix together Dhuwa and Yirritja, Yolŋu and *balanda*, even Tahitian, Indian and African styles. Anything we like!

EG   Kids find new styles by watching videos from far away. That's why they dress up in different costumes. They pick it up on YouTube or Facebook and then they grab it. The next day we see it on a video. That's how they get these things from YouTube. They go in through their phones to pick up ideas.

     Once they find a cool style they start practising. They take their phones to the oval or near the airport. They like to practise in the bush, in clear and quiet areas, copying clothing and styles from YouTube. They mix the styles they find from far away. But it's still our culture. They are joining things together. Making them *waŋgany* [one].

KD   Those dances and videos aren't made for *balanda*. These boys are challenging each other. They're not talking about *balanda* and Yolŋu culture. They're talking about themselves. It's just about the fun; they're not criticising Yolŋu or *balanda*, they're just challenging other *biyarrmak*, funny dancing groups.

     It's all about the challenging: who does the funniest dancing, who is the best dancer in Arnhem Land. They're showing off, showing their *gakal*, their style, to other dancers. It makes them proud, challenging one another so other groups can think about how they beat the others. There's no meaning, no story. Just fun.

WB   They start doing those dance moves in a comical way, like they've seen *balanda* do on shows like *Australia's Funniest Home Videos*. They're making each other laugh. Like on that show.

EG   They watch each other through YouTube, especially the Djuki Mala [Chooky Dancers], but other mobs too. But then they do their own dance. They're not copying. They're finding their own style. Like these boys here who call themselves Wildfree Boys.

KD   *Biyarrmak* makes you wake up and feel alive.

It's not serious. It wakes you up and stops you thinking too much. It takes your mind off things.

PAUL GURRUMURUWUY

This is from a video by some boys who call themselves Gomu Boys. That means Hermit Crab Boys. Before they start dancing they record a message to other boys from other tribes and places: *This is for you from Gapuwiyak. You other boys, wherever you are filming yourselves dancing. You're nothing. You're boring. This is my crew. The Gomu Boys plus one yothu [ritual manager].*

KAYLEEN DJINGADJINGAWUY

Miyalk [women] can make funny *buŋgul* too. That kind of dancing is not only for boys. The women teach themselves different, different kinds of styles.

They dance all kinds of things like emu, heron, fish, seagull, floating log, yam, crocodile, dog, tortoise, yabbie.

They mix Dhuwa and Yirritja to make a funny remix. Just for themselves, or for others laugh with them. There's no meaning, it's all made up. Just for fun. Old people, young people love it. *Wakal buŋgul*, just dancing for fun... anybody can laugh. And no one will get upset.

They might do this *buŋgul* at the community football grand final, or just practice at home for the family.

Here they look like Tahitians because Jennifer bought that stuff on the Internet. So they could look like other cultures, but make it Yolŋu. It's not serious. It wakes you up and stops you thinking too much. It takes your mind off things.

PAUL GURRUMURUWUY

Worlds of pattern are only possible if the pieces that make them up remain in motion.

JENNIFER DEGER

PHONE & SPEAR

PG These days there are lots of colours. How come? I don't know. Up until now you've only seen us use black, yellow, red and white. That's a different type of art. What we're showing you now is a new way of doing art, full of colours, full of fullness, full of meaning. Full of *dhäkay-ŋänhawuy*.

KD Old people got *gamunuŋgu* [ochre paints] and *marwat* [brushes made of hair], *larratkj* [ceremonial painted burial poles], but people now got *bitja bitja* [digital photo assemblage].

I like to do *bitja bitja* with *mayawa* [frilled-neck lizard] or eagle, or sunset and *yiki* [knife] for my mother's Dhalwaŋu clan. Or I get honey and bees to show the Yolŋu life, like real photos of bees or drawings, and then I add in *manikay* [soundtrack] and make-up to make it *yuwalk*, real and alive.

■

JD This phone-made media is concerned with a particularly Yolŋu approach to the work of showing and seeing. Yolŋu understand that to make oneself into an image is to press something into the field of visibility. This showing of oneself is an inherently political act. You are calling attention to yourself, positioning yourself, asserting yourself. Inviting others to look. Offering yourself up to be seen.

At the same time, making and sharing these images involves the cultivation of particular ways of seeing: seeing beyond the image to the deeper layers within it; seeing connections not only between kin, but to images that are not suitable for public display; seeing connections to things that you may not have ever seen before, but which can inhere within an image—even these Google photo assemblages.

PG *Buyayak* is a word we use. It means like it's there, but you can't see it. The old people can see it, the senior members of a tribe.

■

JD For Djingadjingawuy this *bitja bitja djäma* is a way of coming into direct relationship with ancestral knowledge, though in a way and at a level suitable for her age and knowledge base. Through this cut-and-paste assemblage work, she is cultivating her own capacity to see and to know the invisible.

PG   Before mobile phones it was hard for Yolŋu to get hold of *bitja*. We had to rely on *balanda* to make prints and buy frames, or to laminate photos for us and then send them on the barge. We had to go the public phone box and ring someone like an anthropologist or teacher and ask them to send us the DVDs they'd made from our ceremonies, or when we went hunting together. Some Yolŋu did have cameras but it was hard to share the images. Not many people had laptops or iPads. Nobody had printers or even memory sticks.

But then... boom! We had those phones and we could start to make our own *bitja*. We could take photos of our young men at their *dhapi* circumcision ceremonies, or make silly videos of kids and families, just like on *Australia's Funniest Home Videos*.

At that time, the young people started making a new kind of art. They started using their phone to grab photos from here and there and then making them into one *bitja* with colour and patterns. Just like a bark painting, these *bitja* show deep family connections. They connect Yolŋu to the land, the *madayin*. These pictures are full of life. Not dry *gamunuŋgu*, like bark painting. Both tell the same story, but they are different. These are full of colour, brightness and energy.

JD   Through this *bitja bitja djäma* Yolŋu senses become animated and attuned to a more-than-human world of revelation and relationship.

PG   When Yolŋu look at these images they can see connections through the songlines, from the land right up to the sea.

■

JD   Anthropologists often use the term *ancestral power* to identify both the source and subject of Yolŋu creativity. The difficulty with such formulations is that it suggests that Yolŋu art and ritual depend entirely on the creative actions of those who came before. This obscures the degree to which this is a two-way street—the way that formal innovation and contemporary modes of creative engagement can enliven current generations, the old people and country itself.

JG   Before mobile phones, young people had no chance to do this kind of identity *djäma* [work]. They had no chance to sit and make *gamunuŋgu* with the old people. Because they were not allowed to. Maybe they thought we weren't ready. Young people don't paint their *gamunuŋgu* in ceremony. Or on bark paintings. Or other important things.

With the real *gamunuŋgu* it is not allowed for everyone to look and sit and share that pattern. Some *gamunuŋgu* are hidden, not to be shown in public. Some hidden for ever. Most of them. It's only the men that know. Not the young boys or women.

JD   Despite the fact that Yolŋu from neighbouring communities (and even members of the same clan who live in neighbouring outstations) paint variations of clan designs, the Yolŋu families I work with made a deliberate decision, many years ago, not to produce their *gamunuŋgu* as art for sale or public display.

For these Wunun̠murra men the act of *not painting* is a highly political act, and simultaneously a means to conserve ancestral force and to avoid the dangers of scrutiny and retribution associated with what might be seen as reckless revelation.

As Fred Myers has described in a different context of Aboriginal art and display, 'Concealment and control lie at the heart of an Indigenous performance that seeks to impress us with its value without accepting the dominance of those who view.' In this respect it is the considered acts of *not showing* and *not telling* on these pages that arguably does the most to affirm *rom* and its enduring authority. As our commentaries provide *balanda* a glimpse of processes that Taussig might identify as 'the skilled revelation of skilled concealment', it becomes possible to begin to appreciate the twist of tension within each image, as Yolŋu negotiate the making and circulating of images always alert to the possibility of showing too much, or something that one does not have the rights to show at all. This managed tension between revealing and concealing adds to the push-and-pull aesthetic force of each tender assemblage.

PG   Yolŋu way, you have to be careful. If you spit it out—your *gamunuŋgu*, *dhäwu*, *rom*, and everything—you're not to live for a long time.

To make the *bitja*, first thing we do is buy a phone at the community store. Once we've got a phone we can start taking photos of people in all kinds of situations. Or we ask our family to send a picture straight to our phone. Then we start connecting all the photos together, doing the image work. We start planning what we're going to use, like sunset or our totems.

ENID GURUŊULMIWUY

When the young people make those pictures on their phones, what they are doing is making those photographs *waŋa* [talk, speak, ask for]. Yolŋu can hear that call. We can feel it. Those pictures connect us back to the *wäŋa*, to our family and our law, they take us straight there, in our minds, our hearts, our *rumbal* [bodies].

PAUL GURRUMURUWUY

BITJA DJÄMA
Santiago Carrasquilla, 2017
PICTURED
Bambat Ganambarr

This a different way of showing arts through the colours and the reflections. Because colours can talk, nature can talk, Yolŋu can talk, *gamunuŋgu* can talk.

Yolŋu have always had art inside our *rumbal* and our *doṯurrk*, in our bodies and our hearts. What people make depends on their aims, skill and style. With mobile phones we're making a new kind of Yolŋu art. But it still comes from inside. It still comes from Yolŋu *doṯurrk*.

PAUL GURRUMURUWUY

That's *gakal*. That's Yolŋu style.

ENID GURUŊULMIWUY

JD   Along with the right to show comes the capacity to see. At every point in our discussions about these *bitja*, the members of Miyarrka Media were careful to defer to the knowledge and authority of senior members of the relevant clan and their *djuŋgaya*, or ritual managers. As I was told repeatedly, a young person simply will not see what an old person sees in the same image, whether on bark, body or screen-made collage. They just don't have the experience and knowledge to see the levels of meaning that are understood by all to be embedded in these patterns of kinship.

What that means is that young people who make these *bitja* do so with the understanding that even though they may not have the requisite skills or knowledge to paint *gamunuŋu*, with the phone they are able to participate in the making and circulation of a new genre of unrestricted designs: family portraits that are perfectly suitable for public circulation, even though they contain as much story, relationship and sacred significance as a traditional ochre *gamunuŋu*.

∎

JG   When mobiles came in, everything became open. The phone allows everyone to give their picture; to give a *yindi* picture for *bukmak* (everyone, *balanda* and Yolŋu). We can use Blingee with photos instead of painting. The phone can tell the same *dhäwu* but using different techniques. All young people now have a chance to identify themselves through the mobile phone, to show others their totem, their dreaming, their *dhäwu*, through the mobile phone connecting *djäma*. We are using our mobile phone to talk to other people through the images. We show everyone who we are, where we belong, what's our land, or totem, our mind and our power. We can feel proud. And strong. And connected.

∎

PG   Young people these days can be invited into ceremony to see *gamunuŋu*. They can learn to paint, under the supervision of the old people, the owners of that design and the *djuŋgaya*. Because old peoples' eyes fail and they can struggle to paint those fine lines. They need young people to help. So things are changing.

A long time ago only *djuŋgaya* could do that. But we are inviting young people to take that position. It's up to them. Their phones can't do everything.

■

KD   My favourite thing to do on the phone is to keep busy making *bitja*, downloading apps, new-release apps, playing around with *make-up mala*. I don't play games. I don't do Facebook right now, I'm sick of it.

JG   The phone helps young people upgrade their connections. Most people are doing this. Even if you don't know your *gamunuŋgu*, you can see it.

■

PG   Everybody knows that it's not just good things like dancing, music and *bitja* happening through the phones. Bad things come through the phones too. But our work with Miyarrka Media is about showing how kids have learned to use their phones in the right way. In ways that support law, kinship and identity. Having fun and still taking pictures the right way.

This *bitja* thing is just a little thing. But as they get older, they will know through *djalkiri*, *bäpurru*, *manikay*, through the foundation, the clan and the songs.

■

JD   Yolŋu explicitly understand the phone as a conduit, a mechanism that opens one up to social expectations, and therefore as something to be managed, judiciously opened and closed in order to manage the flow of demand or even threat potentially coming down the line.

JG   Mobile phones give young people the chance to connect to their identity, especially if they aren't really sure. Many Yolŋu lost their identity because of drugs. They are not interested in *rom*. That's the true story. Since around the year 2000 too many Yolŋu people are concentrating on drugs.

EG   The way to solve our problems today is to put modern life back into the *rom*. That's what our leaders have to do.

KD   The Yolŋu way of life is to make it real. Not talk-talk. Action has to happen. To make it alive.

PG   This is a Yolŋu way of drawing near, pulling you back to who you are— your *bäpurru*, your *yapa* [your sister clan], your *märi*, your ŋä<u>nd</u>i... these images are about drawing Yolŋu back.

WB   Only the *gamunuŋgu* can identify the person. It gives a big picture, for Yolŋu and *balanda*. These *bitja* made with the phone through Google and the camera, they can help *balanda* to see where we are coming from. If they looked at my *bitja* they could see the Yolŋu picture with the shark and the water and the story. But if they only looked at a painted *gamunuŋgu* they'd have no idea what it represents. Because *balanda* don't know.

      This style is more safe too, no one is going to get in trouble. Phones make it easy, but the images we make are not really serious, they're fun to do and the *dhäwu* is real. Because it is there already, you can see it showing through the picture.

PG   Yolŋu use these *bitja* to see deeper. These are not only outside pictures. They are full of deep meaning and feeling. They tell stories. They show the *rom*.

                                        ▪

JG   There is a lot of politics with *gamunuŋgu*. If you do a painting it can lead to arguments about who owns that *gamunuŋgu* and who has the right to paint it and show it. But on the phone it's clear. The young people just show themselves and their family and their relationship to their *wäŋa*, their *märi wäŋa*, their ŋä<u>nd</u>i *wäŋa*. Whatever they feel like. And no one can argue. Or get upset.

                                        ▪

PG   One man cannot hold all the patterns. You have to be *barrkuwatj* [separate]. You have to be separate. Some men do know a lot for their area and the areas that they are *djuŋgaya*, they are the managers for that *rom*. But the *gamunuŋgu* will always be held separately. They are different. They belong to different people and different *wäŋa*. That's Yolŋu life and Yolŋu politics.

I can't go there and ask for another clan's patterns. Because I don't know. Only the family knows.

•

KD   When the early phones arrived they had different effects already inside to frame our photos. And then when we got the touchscreen phones we could go through Google Play to get *make-up* [visual effects]. We got hold of all kinds of frames and editing apps for our videos and photos so we could make them colourful and patterned, in different ways. All through the phone.

For example, I get some of my photo make-up from the Internet. I download backgrounds when I want something like water, or honey, or a frill-neck lizard. Because I can use that to show where I come from. So I can show my family identity by putting them into the water, or into the honey. After the make-up I will pull it all together with the names or whatever else we want. That's how we make it *waŋgany*, make it one.

Young people, we've got more skills with the phone. What we can do is remix, like taking this new technology and making *bitja* that show our connections in a new way. When I have quiet time, like at night when I have free data because I am good at choosing a good plan, I do my *bitja djäma*. I don't like games or things like Facebook or AirG. I love to make these *bitja*. It is *yuṯa rom*. I love this. I get so excited. I want this and this. I never get tired hands because this work gives me power and strength. This is *yuṯa rom*. Making *yuṯa mala rom* [a new way to live in relation to country and kin]. A new way to be alive and active.

PG   Yolŋu people can share their clothes, their shoes, their TVs... anything really. But they don't share their phones. These are personal things. Other people might use it, sometimes kids will borrow it to play games, but you don't give it to other people to take to other places. Because inside that SIM and memory card is all that person's connections, in the music, the *bitja*, the videos and the phone numbers themselves. It's their identity.

EG   We are Yolŋu. If something bad happens we are always getting our leaders to go into the *rom* and *maḏayin* to give *raypirri*—that's a way of talking to give encouragement and guidance. Sometimes those kids are breaking in, or going to jail, and so the elders bring that Yolŋu and put him to that *rom*. Instead of stopping in jail for two years, or four years, or six years.

Sometimes police take the kids because they've been breaking in, and all our *mala* leaders—the leaders of all the tribes who live here in Gapuwi-yak—phone them up to ask them to bring them back, and we'll have to put them into *rom* and give them a story, about which *manymak* life to lead, which path to follow.

PG   Young people today are just going any which way, but when they get older they will recognise who they belong to. Who is their *yapa*, their *märi*, all this is connected. Connected to the *wäŋa*, to the *gapu*. Moṉuk, *raypiny*, fresh and salt water; and land and nature. Trees. Certain trees have songlines and *manikay*.

·

PG   Older people like me look at the phone as a way to connect to their land, a way to think about their mothers and fathers who have passed away. And they need that phone, because every time they hear their ringtone, it takes them back. Not forward.

·

EG   Sometimes the kids start growling each other through Facebook. All the kids, they jealousing each other. They're provoking each other through Facebook or AirG, which can lead to them fighting each other on the road.

Boyfriend, girlfriend, that's the reason. Lots of times we see them. Then the kids take video of that fighting and put them to YouTube. That's the fun. Everyone can watch. Everywhere. Every time the fight starts, every-one comes down with their phones.

JD   Does that make those kids shamed?

EG   *Bäyŋu* [no, nothing]. They're proud. That's their life. Sometimes we go to the YouTube and watch the kids fighting. Or dancing. Like those other mobs.

JD   Do people put *yätjkurr* [bad] things on the Internet?

EG   I don't know. Because last time the policeman came and checked the phones, for *yätjkurr* things. Sometimes kids are using the phone for *manymak* things, sometimes *bäyŋu*.

.

JD   When Djingadjingawuy talks about the phone as a technology that enables *yuṯa rom*, she is not talking about a new law replacing the old. She is talking about using her phone to enact the values and practices of the past *in a new way*. The technological extension of her projective reach allows her to embody the honey hunter Wurray and so to participate in the making and remaking of the world. In this way, she has accessed what one might call the ancestral affordances of the mobile phone.

.

KD   For a little while, in 2016, I had two phones: an iPhone and a Samsung Galaxy Edge 7. The Samsung was better for the *bitja bitja* work; the iPhone I liked for video. But then my cousin stole my Samsung and my sister's son accidentally dropped and smashed the iPhone screen, so now I'm trying to save money for another phone and have to use my mother's. I did most of these *bitja* on my Samsung.

I jump through the phone and find the elements I need in Google, and bring them back and put them together with the photos I have on my phone, working with my *ŋayaŋu* and *muḻkurr*, my heart and mind. I use colours, frames, family, feelings, names, memories, stories, *manikay*. That's how I make everything *waŋgany*, everything as one. That's how I make it *yuwalk*—alive and real.

JD   Djingadjingawuy's birth certificate lists her first name as 'Kayleen'. But for a few years she preferred to be introduced to *balanda* as Kylie, finding the sound similar, but more pleasing. In the long run this proved difficult, however, as all her official paperwork (like bank accounts and employment documents) insist on her using her 'official name'. So she's given up on Kylie, though I sometimes still call her that. Her family call her Djinga (except her brothers, who are not allowed to say her name).

Djinga and I got to know each other well during the fourteen days of Gurrumuruwuy's wife's funeral. She was one of the kin appointed to look after the body. Djinga was also the one who Yangathu, her *märi*, had

The Yolŋu world is like a
jigsaw puzzle. Everything
fits together. It doesn't
matter how long you run,
how far you drift. The
wäŋa itself will pull
you back. *Gurruṯu*, your
family connections,
will pull you back.

PAUL GURRUMURUWUY

Thinking and worrying and crying. That is *dhäkay-ŋänhawuy rom*, the law of feeling and relationship. You see with your eyes, then you start thinking, putting that *bitja* into your *ŋayaŋu*, your heart, and you start crying. Because you have to start seeing, thinking and feeling like someone is lost.

ENID GURUŊULMIWUY

DJALKIRI, OUR FOUNDATION
Simeon Rigamawuy Wunuŋmurra, 2016

Those four old men, they are in the *djalkiri*, the foundation, the *luku*, the footprint. *Djalkiri* means you are walking with that foundation. It is inside you, in your blood. You are linked.

Djalkiri means that even if something horrible happens, or you get into trouble, you will still come back to the foundation, that anchor.

ENID GURUŊULMIWUY

I know it looks *yut̲a*, but the *manikay* and *rom* are old. Anchor, *yiki* and *ŋarali'* [tobacco]. Birrinydji is the man, the ancestor for us. I heard at Gurrumuru in the special bush area, his *birrimbirr* [spirit] is there all the time. And you can hear that *yiki* in *bäpurru* time with your own ears. It's there. I heard it lots of times. But only when somebody passed away. You can hear over at Gurrumuru. It's there. That *yiki*.

For Gurrumuru and Dholtji, those homelands are connected because of *wetj* [relationship made through a gift between places], connection *waŋgany* [one], *märi-gutharra* [maternal grandmother-grandchild]. Connection through *rom*. I'm talking about the culture. Together in *buŋgul*, the *yiki*. You can dance. It's hard to explain, but it's there.

PAUL GURRUMURUWUY

WURRAY, HONEY HUNTER
Kayleen Djingadjingawuy Wanambi, 2016

If you look at this *bitja*, you can see that's me. I am the one with the spear. Doesn't matter that I'm a *miyalk*, a woman. In this *bitja* I am Wurray, the honey hunter, throwing my spear to the future. I am thinking through that Wurray's spear. Imagining my life.

I made this from *bitja* I collected from the Internet. First I just got any *bitja* of the bush with *gadayka'* trees, those trees that *balanda* call stringybark. Then I started looking for my family on the Internet so that I could put them together in a new way. The photo of my brothers came from images *balanda* put up. I found them through Google.

I have many, many *bitja* on my phone, but I made this one especially to show myself and to show you, *balanda* people, who I am.

When I make this *bitja* showing my ancestral spear on the phone, I'm imagining my own aims and goals. That spear points forward. This *bitja* shows me imagining who I'm going to be, what job I'm going to get, how I'm going to live my life, because I'm young. I don't know my future yet.

I am thinking through that Wurray honey hunter *gara*—underneath I believe in Garray [God], because he's the one who created the world, protecting you wherever you go, shielding, guiding... I feel like home when I go back to Raymaŋirr and I see the water and the sunset and those things that are the foundation of our *rom* and *dhäwu*—I feel present, feel closer to Garray... we got *wäŋa*.

KAYLEEN DJINGADJINGAWUY

WANAMBI FAMILY LOVE
Kayleen Djingadjingawuy Wanambi, 2015

In the centre is Peter, who was the leader of Marraŋu clan until he died in 2018. He was the oldest of all his brothers and held the *manikay* and *rom*. He grew his hair long because of that *dharpa* [tree] we call *djuway*. It represents that Yolŋu at the *bäpurru*, at the ceremony like a funeral.

That frame is holding everyone in the *gapu*. His white and blue represents blue clear water where you get those bubbles. The bubbles coming up from the spring water that you sometimes see in fresh or salty water.

KAYLEEN DJINGADJINGAWUY

From my point of view this is full of meaning. For me that blue-and-white pattern is like the *gapu*, the special water at Raymaŋirr. That *gapu*, that fresh spring water is calling me, calling my name to Raymaŋirr.

For Marraŋu people, the landowners, like Peter and Djingadjinga, every time they go for a swim that *gapu* makes their hair grow. That shows that they are really connected to the *gapu*, the land, the *rom*. That's how people can see that connection.

MEREDITH BALANYDJARRK

TWO WAṉAMBI BOYS
Kayleen Djingadjingawuy Waṉambi, 2015

Two men travelled from Muypan [Goyder River] right up to Raymaŋgirr. Djuway is the name of these two spirit men travelling through the land. The white feathers on their heads represent the *gurrukuwuru gapu muḻmul-mirr*, the fresh water that bubbles up at the shore in our homeland.

This photo was taken two years ago, when Geymul and Djambala graduated from Gapuwiyak school in Year 12. The dot dot on their faces shows the *guku* and the *gapu*, the honey and the water. The black clothing shows their identity with *wäk* [the crow]. The blue colour represents the *gapu*, the water that holds Yolŋu spirits.

The white stripe on their head is the white foam in the calm water that looks like *guku*. We call it *muḻmul* [foam, lather, froth, suds, bubbles]... and it drifts along.

In the picture on the left, they're looking forward into the future. Like the spear. If in your mind you bring in the picture of that Wurray throwing his spear, then that adds to the *dhäwu*. Then there is the reflection on the other side. That's like an olden-day picture, and it shows that when they pass away they will return to the land, to *maḏayin* and *rom*, the sacred objects and way of life. Back to our law.

KAYLEEN DJINGADJINGAWUY

MY WANAMBI FAMILY
Kayleen Djingadjingawuy Wanambi, 2016

BAIRD FAMILY
Kayleen Djingadjingawuy Wanambi, 2015

This is more of my Wanambi family. Wurray is in the middle carrying his spear, a stone axe for chopping down trees and a bag for collecting honey. We were making a video that day, so Banambi grabbed that old axe from the culture centre. The other *bitja* I collected up from different ceremonies.

KAYLEEN DJINGADJINGAWUY

In this one the white colour represents the *guku*. In the middle that's my [uncle] and *mukul* [aunt] and my *gäthu* [nephew]. They all passed away a long time ago.

My *gäthu* passed away about two years ago. I put him in the middle because I love him very much, he's my kind *gäthu*, he always came up to me saying 'Auntie, Auntie, Auntie' giving me hugs and welcoming me, sitting and talking to me.

That's all his brothers and sisters surrounding him. This little boy is taking all our hearts away.

KAYLEEN DJINGADJINGAWUY

The Yolŋu way of life is to make it real. Not talk-talk. Action has to happen. To make it alive.

KAYLEEN DJINGADJINGAWUY

DESCENDANTS OF DJALANDJAL
Kayleen Djingadjingawuy Waṉambi, 2015

This is my grandfather and grand-mother. I put love in the middle because I love my grandmother. I knew her before she passed away, I looked after my grandmother when I was five years old. This hot heart means I still love her *mirithirri mirithirri ḏäl* [really, really strong]. I never forgot her in my life and in my mind. I put chains because they are *dhuyu* [sacred], coming from *baḻaŋu* [anchor]. *Lukuṉur* [coming from the foundation] of my *ŋathi's* [maternal grandfather's] dreaming.

That's all his children. At the top. Only the two in the middle are still alive. And this heart represents them... the second little heart. And that flower represents my mother (aunt, Gurrumuruwuy's sister), Bayni, who passed away a long, long time ago. I never saw her when she was alive.

That flower is me. Djingadjingawuy. And that heart represents me because I never knew my grandfather. Never seen him, I've only seen my grandmother. So that little heart represents that I need her. And that big heart represents what I've got two left from those generations before me: my mum and uncle. The red flower, *wurrki*, is because they are Dhaḻwaŋu. So if you look at it another way, that hot heart represents Gurrumuru. It's like *ŋärra* [ceremony ground]. I can either see this big heart as my Waṉambi *ŋayaŋu*, or as Gurrumuru *ŋärra*.

KAYLEEN DJINGADJINGAWUY

When you die all the elements come in. Like from *märi*, all those elements will come close to you. All the *märi-pulu, yapapulu*, all those clans that you are linked to through your family, through the land. For example, if a Dhuwa person dies, all the Dhuwa people will come close, all the links will come for the ceremony, because this is where you are coming from. Because of the pattern.

The chain shows the songs, land, the ceremonies hold that *rom* tight. It's strong and firm. Locked tight to the foundation. The chain and the anchor connect us to the foundation. To hold it there for the future, no matter how many waves of change come, this will stay forever here, passing from generation to generation through *dhawu, manikay, rom*. The red represents the land and the sparks, you can see the heat and power. Same in that heart, like hot metal. The heart represents the loved ones gone, only two left out of four. The heart also represents the *ŋayaŋu* that's holding the *maḏayin*.

That *ŋayaŋu* shows my *djäl*, that means what I go after, my desire, my decision—what I pull to me because I want it so much. It shows the power of *ŋayaŋu* to pull the family back to the land and to become *waŋgany*.

PAUL GURRUMURUWUY

ŊAYAŊU, MY DEEP FEELINGS AS A DHALWAŊU MAN
Mandy Mandhamawuy Munyarryun, 2014

This man is me. I stand with my *ga-munuŋgu*, my clan designs and colours on my belly. Surrounding me is the colour red, the colour of our clan. The colour comes from my ancestral lands, from the red cloth of the flags that we dance with in ceremonies.

The candle shows the Dhaḻwaŋu fire, see the sparks we call *niḻŋniḻŋ'* everywhere? The red flowers show my *ŋayaŋu*, my deep feelings as a Dhaḻwaŋu man. They show the power of my longings, the deepness of my feelings.

This design is *dhuyu*. That means it is full of power beneath the surface, like the fire in that land. It's all inside, in the veins, in the heart. When you walk, you walk with *gamunuŋgu*... We might all look the same from the outside but the old people recognise who you are through this.

It might be that *balanda* get confused when they see that red wine, because they might not know that Yolŋu can sing and dance stories about alcohol because it belongs to Gurrumuru. But Dhaḻwaŋu people, we know this. Other Yolŋu know too.

Dhaḻwaŋu people sing about *ŋänitji* [alcohol]. So do some other Yirritja people. For us *ŋänitji* is in the songs, in the *rom*. So red wine matches perfectly. But here it looks almost black. So if we look it at that way, it can also show the *märi-gutharra* [grandmother-grandchild] relations

between Dhaḻwaŋu and Warramiri people. The sparkling is the fire, the heat that comes from the land, like the sparks come off something really hot. Red is Dhaḻwaŋu colour. It's the colour of our flag. It's the heat of the *wäŋa*; you can't walk barefoot in that place in Gurrumuru.

PAUL GURRUMURUWUY

When you're drunk you can send your mind back to the *wäŋa*, back to the land... We can make jokes too. You could say, 'Don't rock the boat'. When we drink and start to sway, I say, 'Don't rock the boat'. It's a kind of remix; playing jokes.

We call ourselves the names of ancestors, as if we were in a boat travelling, like that warrior man who came in a ship and threw out his anchor at Gurrumuru.

ENID GURUŊULMIWUY

asked to accompany her when she was flown out to Gove hospital feeling lethargic and having difficulty breathing.

When Djinga arrived at the clinic with her bag packed to accompany Yangathu to the hospital, a nurse shooed her home. 'She's a grown woman. She'll be fine.' That same nurse had to wake the family later that night with the news that Yangathu was dead. Blood tests later determined the cause as melioidosis, mostly treatable if caught in time.

Since that funeral, Djinga has become an integral member of Miyarrka Media, bringing her *bitja*-making skills and resilient optimism to our work together. Djinga laughs when she describes that she uses her phone as a means to hunt and provide for her family. But she's good at it. I've seen her in action when she's stuck in town with relatives who've been drinking for days, leaving her—the sober and resourceful one—to look after her nieces and nephews. At twenty-five years old, she is the youngest member of Miyarrka Media.

Like her uncle, Djinga appreciates that these *bitja* allow for complex spatio-temporal modes of self-projection and emplacement. These temporalities are actually more complex than any idea that the old look back and young people look forward, for Djinga also anticipates a life as a spirit in her country after her death, as well as a place in Heaven, even as she dreams about how her life will turn out.

This kind of associative thinking—or 'seeing as if'—is not only a primary mechanism by which the world is rendered resonant and meaningful; it has been fundamental to Yolŋu ways of engaging foreign ideas in many different arenas.

Yet, as Howard Morphy notes, Yolŋu are not the only ones with a sure grasp of the poetics of association:

> Wilbur Chaseling, the first missionary, began a syncretic dialogue with Yolŋu over religious phenomena—a practice that continues to the present. I can only briefly summarise the process here. From Chaseling's writings we learn that he entered into a process of religious dialogue, drawing attention to differences and similarities between Yolŋu and Christian religious beliefs and practices. He did not dismiss

Yolŋu beliefs or attempt to overturn their cosmology. He respected Yolŋu values and said that he learnt far more from Yolŋu than he was able to teach. A key part of Chaseling's teaching was to draw analogies between Yolŋu religion and Christianity, and one consequence of this may be seen in the continuing ways in which Yolŋu relate aspects of their religious practice to biblical precedents. Ancestral Beings as local heroes take the position of saints, the twelve apostles can be seen as reflecting the division of Yolŋu society into clans, the land-transforming actions of the ancestral beings can be seen as reflecting Old Testament theology and the generalised spiritual concept of *wangarr* can be seen as a manifestation of the one true God.

·

PG   When someone goes hunting and they get that kangaroo in the side—Bang! Dead!—with one shot, one spear, then we call that person *djambatj*. These days those young people are *djambatj* with their phones. One shot, straight where they want to go, through that phone and through the Internet.

KD   Do you know the Yothu Yindi song called 'Mainstream'? You should look it up on the Internet.

When I was in boarding school in Darwin I had an mp3 player with this song on it. I used to listen to that old man from Yothu Yindi sing about reflections. Because by looking in the reflections Yolŋu can get meaning and understanding in their own way. These *bitja* are reflections. In Yolŋu we call them *wuŋuli'* or *mali*. That's why I do those images with the double-up. Because they are like the person and their *wuŋuli'*. That's their reflection, or their spirit.

·

JD   Such images produce a certain depth of field, a temporal field of expansion and contraction that draws history and biography into a frame of enduring ancestral belonging and emplacement. Not only do they assemble families and icons sourced from elsewhere to position Yolŋu in relation to their ancestral identities, they also set up a temporal resonance that gestures to the course of a single human life figured, quite literally, by ancestral forms and forces.

This dimensionality plays out in the visual field where the perspective itself is doubled, creating what can now be seen as a startling perceptual dynamic within the frame: the first perspective is the vertical view of the figures as if seen from a standing position; the second is a horizontal view from above, where we see figures emplaced as if in a funeral sand sculpture, or as spirits arising out of clan waters.

The hum of time. Yolŋu-style.

■

KD Look at the Two Waṉambi Boys *bitja* again, 'cause I'm going to explain more. The circle is like *gapu*, that special water we call *mirriny*. We use that same word to describe the entrance to a bee hive. But the blue and white here, it is showing *gapu* bubbling up. There's lots of meaning there. So when we are looking at this *bitja* of those boys at their graduation, from my point of view its *mayali'mirr*, really meaningful, full of meaning.

That pattern reminds me of when we put dot-dot patterns on our face. For me that's like the *gapu*; that *gapu* is calling me, calling me to Raymaŋgirr. It's like the *gapu* bubbling up: *mirriŋur, ŋurruŋur, muḻmuḻmirr, yarpanymirr*.

Everything is coming up from that *gapu*. Can you see now? *Waŋganygurr* [through one], everything coming up as one. To me it looks like they're bubbling out the *gapu*, standing there proud of their achievements.

■

JD As my collaborators kept reminding me, from a Yolŋu point of view it is the *bitja* themselves that *tell stories*. When we were talking images they would often say, 'This bitja is telling us …'. This formulation not only downplays the interpretive task of the viewer—and indeed the story-telling role of the image-maker—it raises the question of how we might possibly prepare our audience to become receptive to the story-telling agency *of images themselves*. Information, analysis, or even extensive story-telling can never be enough. So the challenge becomes one of fostering receptivity in the viewer. How might we encourage a sensorial, affective and imaginative openness where the images might begin to 'speak to' our readers?

This is where *dhäkay-ŋänhawuy* comes in. With *dhäkay-ŋänhawuy rom* attention is paid to the ways that the audience might be lured closer, past the initial moment of surprise or attraction, to be intrigued, surprised or otherwise sensuously stimulated to open themselves to the potential of being transformed through sensory and imagistic encounter. What is also important is that given their own relative lack of knowledge of the ritual realm, *dhäkay-ŋänhawuy rom* provides a mode of sensory, experiential knowledge and relationship-making that all the members of Miyarrka Media feel confident in claiming expertise.

MB This book will be like a mobile phone—everyone will connect through the book.

JD For the Aboriginal people of east Arnhem Land, there is no necessary, or obvious, correlation between a spear and a phone. This is our own conjunction, our own jaunty juxtaposition, something that Miyarrka Media came up with in the course of making *Phone & Spear*. Yolŋu who are not directly involved in this project will likely be puzzled when they read the title for the first time. But that's partly the point, really. 'They can understand if they think about it,' says Gurrumuruwuy.

WB Nowadays, not many young people are learning how to paint *gamunuŋgu* with ochres. Maybe the leaders won't teach them. Maybe they don't trust them. Maybe there are other reasons. I don't know. But with our phones young people can make *bitja* full of life. Bright. Colourful. Lovely. True. That's the hidden secret.

▪

JD The word 'enargia', Greek for 'visible, palpable, manifest', points to describing things with a sensory vividness. Although it's a term generally tied to language and rhetoric, it seems to me to be a good way to describe what is going on here in a multisensory register.

But, of course, this vividness intensifies and affirms something more than sheer sensation.

▪

KD   Life can be hard. There are a lot of bad things going on in the community, like alcohol, drugs, fighting through Facebook, sorcery and suicide. But I don't think about that. I need to handle my own *rom*. What that means to me is to be strong, to be who you are. Like if you are Marraŋu, if there is a Marraŋu clan ritual, then you should be there always. Dancing. Showing people who you are. Always.

My future is still a long way away... What's going to happen to me? Will I still be walking with that *gara*, with that spear? Or will my future fail? Bad luck? I believe in my heart like that *mokuy* throwing that spear, I believe I will be strong, still going.

That's why I gave you that *bitja* with the *mokuy*, Wurray. So you can catch on.

Only the *gamunuŋgu* can identify the person. It gives a big picture, for Yolŋu and *balanda*. These *bitja* made with the phone through Google and the camera, they can help *balanda* to see where we are coming from.

WARREN BALPATJI

This is an important one. This is me. The frame matches this story perfectly. The colours of red, black, yellow and white match the painting on my belly. The colours in the frame come out of that design. The sparkle there, that is the Dhaḻwaŋu clan fire. You can see the anchor and ŋarrpiya [octopus] from Gurrumuru, the place I am named after. These are outside images for important things. The octopus's eyes are maḏayin [restricted], only men can know the name and the body of the octopus. It changes colours. Just like the sunset. The colour of the ŋarrpiya is like the colour of the sunset. That ŋarrpiya brings colourful sunsets.

In the centre image, I am painted in the design that I hold the responsibility for. It shows my identity, my knowledge, my power. That bitja is of me in Denmark, where they made a statue of my body and gamunuŋgu. This was the first time that a Yolŋu person ever was made into a statue.

The black around the anchor is for the Warramiri people who use the surname Bukulatjpi. They are märi for the Dhaḻwaŋu people, through the ceremony side. The anchor is an important thing for Dhaḻwaŋu people. You might think it's come from balanda, but you would be wrong. That anchor (and that knife) is born in the land. Balanda can't see it, but we know it's there in the land. I know this might be confusing for balanda. But that manikay [song] holds the yiki [knife], anchor, ŋarali', alcohol and other things. Especially for Warramiri and Dhaḻwaŋu people.

When I die, my body will go back to the soil, to the land. But my birrimbirr will remain. That's what the doubling-up of my image or wuŋili' tells you here. I will be gone, but still here, in my clan country as well as in Yalakun and the lands I cared for all my life.

This bitja is also like the sand sculpture that holds a Dhaḻwaŋu body before it goes into the ground. We can build that djalkiri munatha [sand, soil], that special sand sculpture, at funerals for Dhaḻwaŋu people. In Gurrumuru at sunset you can sometimes hear the sound of the octopus that lives under the ground—djatj djatj; it sounds like metal. When you hear that sound it might be telling you that something is coming. Something is going to happen. Maybe someone is going to die.

PAUL GURRUMURUWUY

When Dad's gone we might hear him making the sound of that ŋarrpiya, that octopus. Sounds like this... djatj djatj.

ENID GURUṈULMIWUY

My name is Djingadjingawuy and people call me Djingawuy, or Djinga, for short.

Djingadjingawuy is the name of those yellow flowers from the *gaḏayka*' stringy-bark tree. They are the sweet flowers that the bees fly to, going back and forth to the hive with their sticky sweetness.

In our funerals we dance that *guku* and people hold those leaves. It doesn't matter if there are no flowers at that time. We can dance with the leaves and Yolŋu see that the flowers are there. Or sometimes we will use other kinds of flowers, doesn't matter if they are other colours or from the shop. Yolŋu will still see that lovely yellow *djingadjingawuy*.

KAYLEEN DJINGADJINGAWUY

Happy Valentine

DHALWAŊU FAMILY
Raelene Warrinydhun Garmu, Mandy Mandhamawuy Munyarryun,
Kayleen Djingawuay Waṉambi, Santiago Carrasquilla, 2017

See how everything comes together?
There is pattern, story, family and
deep, deep meaning here.

When you are dealing with serious
things like this, I don't think of it as
remix. When you get closer to the old
people and their way of seeing, then
you don't joke around.

PAUL GURRUMURUWUY

LUKUWURRŊU
Mandy Mandhamawuy Munyarryun, 2014

My daughter Balanydjarrk is named after that anchor Lukuwurrŋu. She is coming from the foundation of the anchor. The red colours show her Dhal̲waŋu identity. Even when she's travelling around, this picture shows that she's still rooted in the land. And you get that feeling of power coming from that land, from the waters in our land, the waters where her spirit will return one day.

The land of the Dhal̲waŋu people has such heat, power, energy and strength. There's a special sound when we sing about the anchor dropping. See the ripples going out? It reflects the Dhal̲waŋu woman and al Dhal̲waŋu people.

PAUL GURRUMURUWUY

BAL̲AWUKU GIRL
Jessica Ganambarr, 2015

Katrina Dharraganmarttji is showing people who she is because of the colour and the *yiki* [knife] shining on her *nirrpu'* [top of her head]. It tells us that she is really a Balawuku girl from Gurrumurru. Balawuku is a way of showing Dhal̲waŋu clan and Wunuŋmurra identity.

Sometimes when you see Dhal̲waŋu people dance, you see that power come through, you see the image of the old people. When the old people are gone you can see their image in the new generation, even in these pictures.

I think that Dharraganmarttji looks serious here because most of our old people, the fathers and the brothers, they looked serious when they got together for ceremony.

MEREDITH BALANYDJARRK

The colours connect you to the land, the songs, and to the people. The colours are related like people. Songs too. It's the most powerful thing. In these photos we get more energy, more power, by bringing together all the different elements.

MEREDITH BALANYDJARRK

2_BROTHAZ_ARGUING 2_BROTHAZ_ARGUING

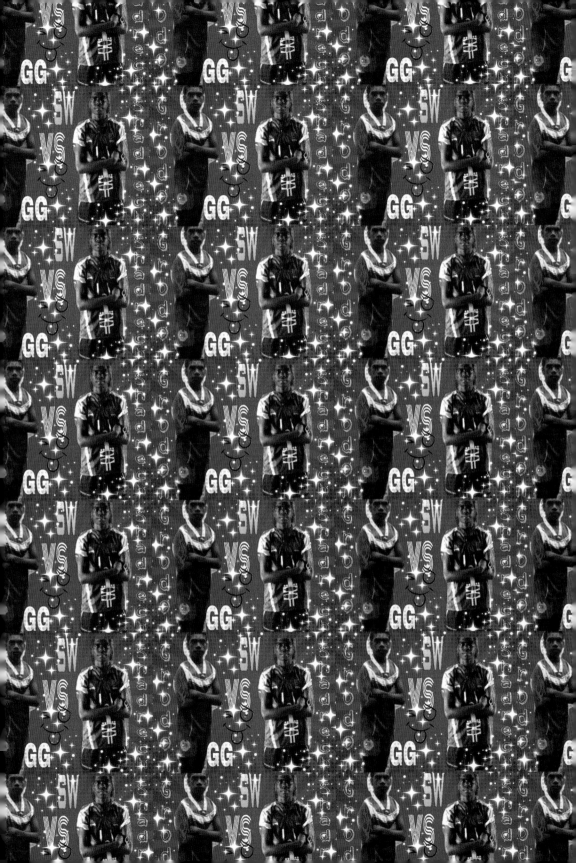

2_BROTHAZ_ARGUING

w are you my dear little brother?

Very very well.

Shall we sit down?

Come. Look at this painting.

It's our sacred clan design.

Really?!

ho's going to look after it ? You?

I already have many
sacred responsibilities

So you should have this one.

So what have we got?

Check out what Dad left us.

Hang on. Let me look.

What?

I'm the senior law man.

But we need to check
who the design really belongs to

tell you it belongs to us. You and me

What's your problem?

We need to take it to an exper
djungaya (ritual manager).

But I'm a ritual expert.

If we don't consult our djungaya
we will both by killed by sorcery.

We can't mess with ancestral la

I'm the ritual leader for our clan.
I stand at the centre.

Yes, I know. You do that all the time.

Just wait!

Jason Marpangar Dhamarra<u>n</u>dji made this one. He's from Ramingining, but people from Gapuwiyak got hold of this video too. I remember, everyone was watching and laughing, passing around the phone.

Jason made the whole thing on his phone, using funny voices in Yolŋu *matha* to make a new story from the *balanda bitja*. We translated it for the exhibitions. It is really, really funny in Yolŋu *matha*.

Jason did both voices. He recorded the *bitja* from a TV set playing a video cassette that had belonged to his *ŋathi*; it was his grandfather's *bitja* but he made this *yu̱ta, biyarrmak* one. He was the first to do these funny voices, showing these *balanda* like they were Yolŋu. Long time ago now.

KAYLEEN DJINGADJINGAWUY

There were many videos like this in the beginning. But these days there's not so many. They used to be passed phone to phone on those old-model phones, before we got Google connections. People are watching YouTube now.

PAUL GURRUMURUWUY

LONELY NYIKNYIK
Tristian Wathangani Munyarryun, 2010
Video Stills

We call this boy Lonely Nyiknyik
here because he is usually with two
other boys all the time. They're the
Nyiknyik gang, named after the bush
mouse. But here he is by himself,
filming himself singing 'Baby', that
Justin Bieber song, in a funny way to
make everybody laugh.

KAYLEEN DJINGADJINGAWUY

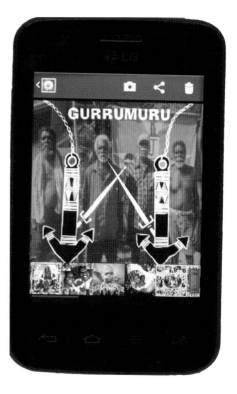

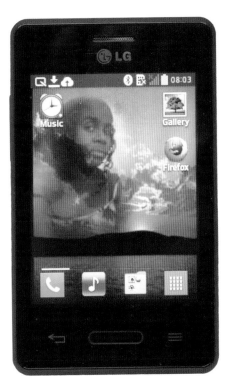

WORRY

KD   Sometimes in the community when there's a lot of trouble, with shouting, that's when you see people smashing their phone. Then straight away they're running to get a new one, with a new SIM card.

·

JD   I love it when my Yolŋu friends tell me stories of people smashing their phones. I can relate to this, though I'm too timidly middle class to follow suit. Over the years, Gurrumuruwuy and I have talked a lot about new stresses that phones have brought and about the ways the phone becomes a way to exert pressure on others from afar; to claim the reciprocities and responsibilities of kinship, even when one is physically far away and *barrkuwatj*.

PG   Sometimes you have to do this, *gäthu*. It's the life; in the city especially, it's hard: you've got to find *rrupiya* for your food and *ŋarali'*. Sometimes it's raining, hard, sometimes you have nowhere to go, your phone gets wet, you get sick, you sleep in the toilet block. That's how it goes. That's the Yolŋu life. And that's when you have to put pressure on people to help you. You ring them up, maybe even threaten to curse them, if you have to, to make them know you're serious. But then again, they are family. They should help you. They can help you.

Other times it might be people ringing you up. When they're stuck, or if they need money for anything. It's hard that way too. Pressure coming from all directions and you're in the middle. In the old days, we used to just be by ourselves, in little groups, not in contact with all these people and their needs and desires. I'm like you; sometimes you just have to hide.

·

KD   Yolŋu ring my phone, lots of times. Sometimes I don't pick up, but if I feel like picking up, I'll answer. Sometimes it's like an emergency call, a family *mari*, like a fight or argument. Sometimes I pick up fast and sometimes ignore. Sometimes it's nothing, sometimes it's bad news.

·

KD   Yolŋu life can be hard. What Yolŋu can do? Ringing, ringing, ringing a lot of times. All the time ringing. Sometimes asking. Sometimes bad stories.

Sometimes saying isn't this weather lovely, how are you feeling?

They can express the feeling that they miss someone else in their family. Like Jennifer, for example, she is in the Djalkiri family, her *wäwa* was working with her. So Susan will ring her up to ask how she is, because she is close to them. That's why Yolŋu feel comfortable with her.

■

JD   I received news of Yangathu's death sitting on the floor of the West Village apartment I'd found for rent on Craigslist. My partner had skyped me. My US phone number put me out of reach of my Yolŋu networks. In my shock I kept repeating, 'but we only just spoke', though it had actually been about 30 hours since I'd called her from the airport in Brisbane before removing my Australian SIM card. We'd spent the previous few weeks together in Darwin editing a film about death, sorrow and the joy of Christmas, and I had just returned to New York.

■

JD   Six years later, Yangathu's superannuation payout was finally transferred into Gurrumuruwuy's bank account. It had taken that long for me to find the time to pull together all the documentation necessary, including signed statements from all her children that they would not make a claim on the funds. Because Yangathu and Gurrumuruwuy had never been officially married by the state, and his name did not appear on her death certificate, we needed letters signed by community elders, and affidavits witnessed by the local police, to attest to their relationship.

The family initially anticipated a generous payout. Yangathu had worked at various times in her life as a part-time clerk working for MAF Airlines and also as an assistant at the community school. At one point the family was convinced that she had accrued a small fortune—I was told with some certainty the paperwork said that there was $400,000 in her account—it turned out, however, when I finally talked to someone at the superannuation fund on speaker phone with everyone listening, the final figure was little more than $8,000.

Even that kind of money doesn't often land in Yolŋu accounts. ('Unless you get royalty money', as Gurrumuruwy corrects me.) It had arrived at a good time; this was the Christmas break and Gurrumuruwuy was in Darwin, taking time out from his work as a ranger, and so he could use it to rent an air-conditioned room at a motel situated between his new wife's mother's housing commission flat and the casino.

It took only five days for Gurrumuruwuy to spend it. I know this because I used an app on my smartphone to help him transfer the money to the account from which it could be accessed.

We spoke many times as I helped him navigate Internet bank transfers. Once he rang in the evening, needing more cash. 'I'm having a party,' he told me. 'I went shopping for oysters and fish.' ('I hate stingy people,' he'd told me a few weeks before. 'You were stingy once, but not anymore.')

On the sixth day, when the bank account was once again empty, he phoned to tell me that he'd spoken to his boss back in Gapuwiyak and that he was due some holiday pay. Might I lend him a little to tide him over until he flew back home?

I laughed, but quickly shut up when he told me in a stern and slightly hurt voice, 'Don't laugh at your father.' He went on to say that I was the only daughter he could rely on; that he would pay me back once he got paid. I knew that this was a version of the truth and that he would pay me back because he managed to live very cheaply at the outstation and so always did. In the end.

I told him that the reason for my laughter was because we were both in the same predicament: my account was empty too (plus I had $24,000 owing on my visa card from a Miyarrka Media art project from the previous year). And in that moment, that was my truth. But, as we both also knew, if I really tried, I could easily find the money for him.

'What's the word for that *warrakan* [bird] that eats animals, leaving only the bones?' he asked.

'Vulture?' I suggested.

'Yes. Vulture. That's what they did to me, *gäthu*. When I got that money, Yolŋu came from everywhere. '*Gurrupul, gurrupul, gurrupul*, give me, give me, give me'. Day and night. They didn't stop. They are still coming, but

I'm only bones. I'm going to ring up that bank and let everyone listen on the speaker, so when they tell me the balance in all my accounts, they can hear that I have nothing. That's the only way they are going to believe me and leave me alone.'

Even though I promise to help him out in a couple of days when I am next paid, Gurrumuruwuy ends the conversation with one final attempt at breaking my resolve, so that he might get the *rrupiya* he needs that same day.

'Think about it, *gäthu*,' he says, referring to me in our kin relationship, as he always does. 'Think about it.'

He uses this expression so that I don't have to say no, and in so doing, refuse the relationship. It leaves things lingering, the connections opened by the phone still in play.

■

JD In 1995, Raymattja Marika-Mununggiritj and Michael J. Christie co-authored a short yet remarkable paper in the *International Journal of the Sociology of Language* entitled 'Yolŋu Metaphors for Learning'. The two educators talk about the cultivation of forms of attentiveness that enable Yolŋu to identify and follow animal tracks in the environment as a necessary precursor to understanding 'the clouds and the tides, the animal tracks and the flowers, the clan totems and the sacred designs, and the songs that have come from the creation'. Although they don't use this terminology, what they point to in this article is a dynamic process of sensuous world-making in which acts of envisaging, making visible and recognising provide key moments in an ongoing project of participatory and relational poiesis.

They talk also about the role of what we in *Phone & Spear* have been calling remix. They write: 'Yolŋu education is learning to love and understand our homeland and the ancestors who have provided it for us, so as to create a life for ourselves *reworking the truths we have learned from the land and from the elders, into a celebration of who we are and where we are in the modern world*' [my emphasis].

■

JD   Thought on a plane: I don't want to write a book about digital technologies. I want to write about love. Or rather *with* love. *From* love. And *into* love. Whatever that means. I make a note to myself, open my novel and fall asleep.

        I don't mean romantic or a romanticising love; what preoccupies me is something more akin to familial love; something foundational, intimate and binding, but always, necessarily, fractious at some level. I want love as a prism through which to consider the relationships that matter in this book.

        I also intend love as a verb, as it infuses acts of care and attentiveness, as it shapes the contours of our lives.

·

JD   In Marika-Mununggiritj and Christie's account, love is not a terrain of interpersonal vulnerability. It is the result of careful cultivation. One arrives at a relationship of love through a sustained attention to the land as site and source of ancestral connection. Love accompanies understanding. It is emergent. It is located. It offers a more-than-human embrace.

·

JD   Inspired by the repeated declarations of love made sometimes in words, but mostly in the heart-shaped motifs adorning so many of the images—and indeed the tender care evidenced in both the making and the viewing of these images—I began to wonder if love might provide the thread to link the stories and experiences I had accrued over twenty years of working with one community—one extended family, really. Could using love as a touchstone of what matters here help me to attend better to the orchestrated moments of affective coalescence that make the state of becoming *ŋayaŋu waŋgany* so socially significant? And so valued.

        After all, love takes me to hostels and hospitals, shopping centres and Centrelink, casinos and funerals, drawing me into versions of life that extend beyond the human: versions of life and relatedness that include ancestral bees and God and digital light.

        Love, I thought, might offer a means to circle back and reposition myself within the work of intercultural recognition that has compelled me for so many years. This is because love teaches you about incommensurability. Not to mention frustration and vulnerability. It schools you in the ways that closeness may lead to friction and, sometimes, irreparable fracture; the ways that we lurch towards and away from each other. Sometimes it's more elegant and orchestrated than that, but the movement is backwards and forwards, it turns on moments of connection *and* disconnection.

A few weeks later, I email a friend who confesses to writer's block, or perhaps something more specific, a kind of resistant freeze against academic language and the ways that our jobs seem to hang on a capacity to pump out words. She asks me if I have any suggestions. I do. I tell her to stop trying to write. I then blurt out my own desire to write differently and my growing attachment to 'love' as the touchstone for this project. She doesn't write back.

∎

JD Still, the idea of love—or rather the amorphous, alluring and reassuring feeling it provided as a way to both claim and characterise the intensified attachments and acts of care that compel me—continued to haunt me as both motivation and mode. Might love, I wondered, offer a means to overcome the distancing deemed necessary for anthropological analysis? As described earlier, *yuṯa* anthropology presupposes a willingness to eschew the academic tendency towards safe detachment and cool appraisal.

Indeed, my Yolŋu family presume that their family photographs cannot make a claim on others unless the viewer brings their own affective associations to bear, their own histories of attachment, their own experiences of familial loss. Taking love, rather than 'the digital', as a touchstone for the project seemed to a way to write more intimately about the media and their makers—myself included—to allow both for our ambitions and our failings in such a way that the aesthetic acts of care, commitment and connection at the heart of this book could be foregrounded without producing a heroic narrative of what Melinda Hinkson calls 'technological redemption'.

Thinking about separation, connection and love, Rebecca Solnit draws on Simone Weil, who writes: 'Let us love this distance, which is thoroughly woven by friendship, since those who do not love each other are not separated.' Solnit goes on to describe Weil's sense of 'love as the atmosphere that fills and colours the distance between herself and her friend'.

How could I not take this snippet to heart?

·

JD My thoughts on love, and the passionate reach of projective association, proved sustaining for a while. But, in the end, I abandoned the idea, fearing it was bad anthropology: the notion of love was too generic, too bound up in *balanda* concepts and expectations.

Instead, I began to focus once again on the images at hand, and to listen more closely to the words that came down the phone line. My Yolŋu kin often say 'I love you' at the end of our phone calls, but if I've been overseas, or out of touch for some time, or if it's a special holiday like Christmas, when they first ring, they will sometimes say they've been worrying for me. It's a way of saying they've missed me. But there's more to it than that.

·

EG When someone passes away we ask family to send a *bitja* to our mobile and then we look at our phone and cry.

Thinking and worrying and crying. That's *dhäkay-ŋänhawuy rom*, the law of feeling and relationship. You see with your eyes, then you start thinking, putting that *bitja* into your *ŋayaŋu*, your heart, and you start crying. Because you have to start seeing, thinking and feeling like someone is lost.

After that I save that picture in my phone so I can think with my heart and my mind whenever I want, going way back to how we spent time with that person who passed away.

·

JD *Warwu* is the word Yolŋu use when they talk about the effects these photographic collages are intended to produce. *Warwu* refers to an active kind of sorrow; it entails a deliberate attention to the gaps produced by absence. *Warwuyun* is to worry for someone or something. It's an emotional state that people deliberately trigger in order to feel into; a properly deep affective space of resonance that opens you up to others through a deliberate foregrounding of separation. It seeks out and cultivates a very particular register of connection, but one that is active, dynamic, enlivened by the push-and-pull life lived as an always unfolding process of connection and disconnection in which one participates in inward as well as outward ways.

Warwu [the noun form of *warwuyun*] is more than an emotional state of being. It's something people do, a kind of *djäma*; it is a word describing deliberate acts of memory, imagination and feeling that involve calling to mind faraway people and places. *Warwu* entails orientating oneself in a specific direction with a specific intent; it requires an opening to the feelings that arise from the fact of being separated, of being apart—all with the expectation that this often-difficult process has a socially transformative effect. Unlike its poor English equivalent, worry, *warwu* is necessary, positive and productive. It might be an internal process, but it is neither individual, nor private *djäma*.

.

PG   When Yolŋu put hearts into those *bitja* they are showing their feelings, they show that they are worrying for their family. But another way you can see those *doturrk* is like something sacred. Like *madayin*. Because Yolŋu hearts are an inside thing, they hold that deep connection to the *wäŋa*, through the *madayin* and the *rom*.

.

KD   A long time ago, Yolŋu didn't do this. But now they've changed, or remixed it.

Back then when someone passed away you couldn't look at *bitja*, or couldn't say their name. But these days you can look at photos and videos and pull those loved ones *räli* [towards you], bringing them closer to your heart and mind. Before, people had to be careful; they put that photo in a suitcase or safe area, until after two or three years when you can look or give it to family. My grandmother was thinking that way. At that time my family didn't have cameras.

Now, if someone passes away they just put that picture in the phone, thinking, reflecting, remembering what they were doing in their life-time. You still can't say that name. But these days people feel closer with their pictures in their phone.

My auntie passed away a little while ago. I still go to her number on my phone. I don't want to delete it. I need to look at that number... to bring her closer, as if she were alive... it would hurt to delete it. I need to see her number and feel close.

JD   Taboos regarding looking at photographs of the dead changed in the early 2000s. Whereas once images of the deceased would have been deemed highly dangerous, now they are valued for the connections that they evoke, so when someone dies, their family start sorting through their photographs, collecting them on their phones, looking at them, stroking them, sometimes talking to them.

Photographs have become an essential element in funerals, often taped to the wall to make patterns of kinship, as was the case at Yangathu's funeral. They then become the backdrop for more family photographs.

Through these processes, the photographic traces of the dead that a previous generation feared as unruly and potentially dangerous become a source of comfort and communicative potential. Arranged alongside their loved ones, located in their homeland, they no longer pose a threat, nor make demands of the living. Instead, as family members will often point out, they *show themselves* as happy.

In the making of these collages the subjects on the screen become united not only thematically and visually, but ontologically, in the sense that otherwise quite distinct and disparate things—categories of things that would normally be separate because of the very nature of what they are, or where they came from, or whether they are living or dead—assume a certain correspondence.

Deeply sentimental, the images shown here strike complex chords. The layered bling of the 'happy' lights signal depths beneath the surface. While the application of such glowing effects might act as a kind of balm to grief and loss, the assembling of the photographs entails a wilful scratching at the wound of loss: the allure of the lights dependent on a deeper willingness to not look away from death itself. (And it's not just through photographs that Yolŋu spend time with death. Their funerals often last two weeks or longer, during which time family members live in close proximity to the coffin and the metamorphosing body within.)

■

JD   A Yolŋu aesthetics of shimmer brings forth the twinned forces of resonance and rupture. For those who know how to peer into its depths, the lights sparkle with a gesture towards an intimacy with lives in which death, beauty and danger comingle; lives in which the withholding of image and information is as crucial as their release; generating the sensuous grounds of poiesis, while simultaneously demarcating the oscillating limits of what can be known, seen, shown, felt and shared.

Over the past thirty years, anthropologists have schooled art lovers to recognise the aesthetic effects of light in Yolŋu art as a manifestation of 'ancestral power'. But what we are invited to experience here is something less abstract. Through the shimmering effect for which Yolŋu have become so well known, the surface of the visible is simultaneously intensified and made permeable. Made to oscillate not only with light effects but also with photography's unique capacity to make absence present, the screen-image becomes porous: a site of emergence. As with the shark pressing up and out of the water, we get a sense of the image itself pushing through into visibility, a sense that the photograph's true subject lies somewhere beneath the surface of the visible.

PG   *Warwuyun* is important. We worry for all our family members we are separated from. Photographs are good for *warwuyun*.

Family collect those sunsets because they bring out heavy meanings and feelings. That's why they look for a sunset shot when someone has passed away. They bring in the other elements that are connected to their clan and it shows that relationship and all the worry that they feel for that person.

■

JD   During the fourteen days of Yangathu's funeral, a vase full of red silk roses sat on each side of her bed. When, on the final day, her children and other *djuŋgaya* danced around her coffin as it was carried to the burial site, dancing as bees darting back and forth, they held these flowers in their hands. They danced with the flowers because it is the scent and sweetness of those flowers that draw those honey bees close as they seek food. Even though these were red roses, everyone there knew how to see them as the yellow flowers of the *gaḏayka'*. But in the same moment, everyone could see that these flowers were red, single-stem roses. Red for their hearts as Dhaḻwaŋu women. Red for their love and longing. Red for the blood of Jesus. Red for their *warwu*. Red for their *ŋanayngu* and *maḏayin*.

They danced with her white coffin, which, in that moment, was recognised by all as a fallen *gaḏayka'*: the fallen 'mother' tree that once held the hive, meaning that the bees have to leave and find another home. The back-and-forth dancing expressed the longing to stay, and the necessity to go.

·

KD   We add in the lights to show that our lost loved ones are happy.

JG   That light, *djarraṯawun'*, it's like a flash, it makes a picture look good. We use that word for any light, like normal light flashing, spotlight, car light, traffic light or bed light. Any light, really, but adding it to picture, that makes Yolŋu feel worry or feel *manymak*, happy. That light brings it to life. When you see the added light, you might feel excited, or shocked, while you worry... *Yä*... that's what you say... We use the light to do that drama.

·

JD   I'm always inclined to transcribe *yä* as 'yaaaaaaaaaa' to capture the way the word opens outwards on an extended breath. The Yolŋu dictionary translates this common Yolŋu expression as: 'Ah! Oh yes! Expression of discovery.'

Shirley Nirrpurranydji, the former principal of Gapuwiyak School, explained *yä* to me while she was staying with us in Cairns after the funeral of her murdered son. '*Yä* is what we say when everything comes rushing back. Or, it can be what you say to photographs. *Yä* is really a feeling. Sad maybe. A word you use when you've got a feeling of missing. Sometimes relief, too. The relief of missing. You say it to the picture, and it then it touches your heart and *muḻkurr* and it all comes rushing back. You say it to whom or what you've been missing. Sometimes with a shake of the head.'

PG   That long sound shows that you are making the connection. The sound will come out in different moods. It can be so sweet, even though you are really missing that person.

·

PG   *Ŋayaŋu* is another word for *maḏayin*.

JD   Heart—not the actual organ, but a word used to refer to the inner, embodied location of feelings—is another word for sacred object.

PG   Our sacred objects are the *ŋayaŋu* of the tribe. So, for example, in funerals Dhaḻwaŋu people sometimes give a special object that will go inside the coffin. And do it gladly. That's our *ŋayaŋu*.

        It is the same on the last night of a funeral. People give their *ŋayaŋu* in the *manikay*, in the song. You can feel it. It's like that *balanda* expression 'from the bottom of your heart'. It's like we are giving out from the bottom of our *rom*.

        Ŋayaŋu is when you give it out gladly. No holding back. Showing who you are through the depth of your feelings.

·

JD   To gloss the light effects of shimmer as 'ancestral power' is to miss so much. By using light effects to transform the visual into a field of flux and sensuous connection, the dynamic of revelation and concealment, showing and withholding, at the heart of Yolŋu knowledge, sociality and politics, becomes materially manifest. The tremulous surface of the visible becomes a site for a sensuous and participatory poiesis.

        Yolŋu understand that it is in the moment that the light begins to infuse the surface of an image that the agency of the artist is usurped, or at least rendered less significant, as the potency of immanent ancestral forces are brought forth and made visible. Places and beings are not merely represented: they show themselves. Viewers feel the effects, they look deep into the image, seeing and feeling their way back to the land.

PG   Your *ŋayaŋu* belongs to that place and you, yourself, every Yolŋu, has to make that connection, that deep connection through feeling. That way your *ŋayaŋu* can sit in that *wäŋa*.

JD   To talk about *ŋayaŋu* is to talk about longing and belonging.

•

EG   Even if we're living in another community, we'll still have to worry for the place we have left, we'll have to go back to that place. Even if we go to another place, we're still worrying for Gapuwiyak.

WB   You have to be careful. If Yolŋu think too much in this way, they can get sick. Too much *warwuyun* is no good.

PG   When you see people sitting on the *djäpana*, the sunset, you see everything: through the feeling and through the imagination, because your *muḻkurr* just opens up, that's how people *warwuyun* through that *miny'tj*, using those colours to think about that family who have passed away. Who is far away, and who is close. That's how I see it. As your eye gets closer, you'll see the family. Not just those photos.

JG   Sunset tells that it's time to worry. It's time to look out for your children who might be out playing, time to call them to come home. Or if your family goes to live at another place, you think of them at sunset.

•

JD   For a long time, I thought of *warwuyun* as a particular and practised capacity to stay with the wrench of separation, opening up to the full devastation of death, and thus enabling Yolŋu to work through their grief in socially prescribed ways. I envied this capacity to literally look death in the face, over and over. It has taken me a long time to realise that it is not actually death that is being looked in the eye and held close.

Gurrumuruwuy's second daughter's husband, James Ganambarr, set me straight: *Warwuyun*, he told me, is a way of feeling good. It is not about death, but life. Life and its capacity to restore, renew and connect.

JG   When you *warwuyun* with these images you 'see those lost loved ones as in life'.

JD   You couldn't have a clearer statement about the generativity of vision: you see loved ones as in life, not as if they were alive. This distinction makes all the difference to what I understand James to mean: he is describing a process of feeling-envisioning that has an animating effect, positioning both subject and viewer within an encompassing field of aliveness and spectral visibility. It is an act of seeing invisible presences—a form of projective imagining of spirits who, in turn, are wanting to show themselves to you.

The effect of this push-and-pull of affect and perceptual agency is that, to a Yolŋu eye, the people in the *bitja* are present as an animating force in the world. In other words, *warwu* entails first recognising, then mediating against, separation. One does not dwell in disconnection.

JG   When you *warwuyun*, your feelings change from worry to something good. Just like the colours change and become beautiful in the sky.

If you keep thinking, thinking, you'll get sick. So you should look, satisfy yourself and put it away. *Nhäma, warwuyun*, look, cry and feel. *Manymak.* Good. Then put that *bitja* away.

DHALATJ BIK
Celina Walmandji Yunupingu, 2013

Mindharr is the name for the green co-lour of the Wangurri clan. This colour is often shown through the green flag in ceremonies.

In this *bitja* it shows us that this Wangurri woman's spirit has returned to her land. No more pain, no more suffering. The lights show she's happy.

Can you see the blue background around her? It looks like water. Maybe the lights represent the sparkling water. There's a Wangurri expression, *dhalatj bik*, that refers to calm water after flood. Here that meaning extends to 'rest in peace'.

MEREDITH BALANYDJARRK

God made us the same. There is nothing different between Yolŋu or *balanda* from my point of view.

ENID GURUŊULMIWUY

DJÄPANA
Kayleen Djingadjingawuy, 2015

Djäpana means sunset. The red clouds called *rreypa* show our Dhal̲waŋu identity. They show the colour of Garray *maŋu'*, God's blood. When we sing *djäpana* it connects us to other Yirritja clans through the songlines. When we see a brilliant red sunset like this it tells us that the sun is going down without someone.

This picture represents our sister clan and also Dhal̲waŋu, Birrkili Gupapuyŋu at Yalakun and the island across the water. This connection comes through the songlines. This *rreypa*, the colours of the sunset in the sky, reflecting with the *galuku* [coconut] floating in the water, hits the water *muŋurru'* (that's the special water that Dhal̲waŋu and Birrkili sing that flows from Gurrumuru).

My youngest sister Wuluku is always complaining that she wants to go back to Yalakun. Every day she says, 'I want to go back. It's boring here.' In this picture it's like she's looking down from the hill at Yalakun. She's where she wants to be. Going fishing by boat and camping. That coconut palm on her shirt represents the Garawirrtja people who are the landowners at Yalakun. We call that *wäŋa yapa*, it's our sister country. It's where we grew up, it's the country we care for, the place our fathers established, the place my mum is buried.

When I go to Yalakun I can feel the *wäŋa* is calling for me. When you go away from the *wäŋa* you can still feel it, because the *wäŋa* is calling. It's calling my mind and my spirit. It doesn't matter that my homeland is Gurrumuru: deep in my heart is Yalakun. I hear that voice not in my ears, but in my heart. It gives me confidence, that land. When I get to Yalakun I will feel confident from that *wäŋa*. All my worries will be gone. I will feel at home.

When I worry for Yalakun I put on the laptop and find that recording of our brother singing Garraparra. That's the one *manikay* that Dhal̲waŋu people can sing to Yalakun. It's part of the songline from Garraparra that links Yalakun. I imagine and it draws me back, to make me feel *manymak*. I feel good then.

When Yolŋu look at a photo they can straight away see all these connections and colours. It hits you. The colours connect you to the land, the songs and to the people. The colours are related like people. Songs too. It's the most powerful thing. In these photos we get more energy, more power, by bringing together all the different elements.

MEREDITH BALANYDJARRK

MAN'JTARR [FLOATING LEAF]
Rowena Laypu Wununmurra, 2011

WÄŊAŊURA [THE PROMISED LAND]
Artist Unidentified, 2013

This is a story about a family still missing their father and husband ten years after his death. The coloured leaves show that he loved reggae music. Lucky Dube was his favourite. It also shows the connection to *man'jtarr* [floating leaf]. It's a way to show that he liked to smoke *waymi* [marijuana]. That little fire in the bottom corner is like the one Yolŋu burn when someone passes away, to cleanse the spirit. Different clans have different names for this.

Bäŋgana was my *wäwa*, the brother who adopted me, my closest kin and collaborator until he died of what the coroner deemed a heart attack, though his family thought otherwise, in 2001, aged thirty-seven.

JENNIFER DEGER

This couple have both passed away now. Joe Ŋalandharrawuy Garawirrtja died in 2009. He was a minister. We used to call him *Bäpa* [Father] Joe. He and his wife, Nimanydja Ganambarr, were both Christian so we see them here in a Paradise Land, or *wäŋaŋura* [the promised land]. The gold especially represents this.

The hearts show their children missing them. The flashing lights show the feelings of love, sorrow and joy that rise up when we see this picture. We can see that they are in Heaven and that they are happy.

MEREDITH BALANYDJARRK

NEVER FORGOTTEN
Kayleen Djingadjingawuy Waṉambi, 2015

MINY'TJI OF THE ṈARRPIYA
Kayleen Djingadjingawuy Waṉambi, 2015

Margaret Mary Marlumbu Waṉambi died around the year 2000. She was my mother's mum. I found her photograph in one of my sister-in-law's photo collections and grabbed it with my phone.

I made this picture to show that old woman's spirit returning to her clan waters. The light shows the special water. Heaven too. That long white cloud is the same as the white feather *raki'* [string] called *malka* that we wear at funerals and use in the ceremony to guide the spirits of the deceased back to their homeland. We point to the homeland with this *raki'*.

The seagull is called Gakararr, it always stays at the beach. Through the *manikay* we see it at Raymaŋirr. It cries for our lost loved ones.

KAYLEEN DJINGADJINGAWUY

I made this *bitja* so that I could think about and worry for my *märi*, Fiona Yangathu, who passed away in 2011. This one shows *yothu-yindi*, it shows the relationship between mother and child. You can tell by the colours. Green for her mother, that fresh water from Dhälinbuy, and that black representing her mother from Dholtji. The circles show her connection to her mother from Dholtji, they reflect the colours of her octopus identity. Two mothers. One fresh and one salt water. That water started from Dhälinybuy and goes to Dholtji because they gave each other the agreement to give each other the *gapu*. So this picture tells about the *riŋgitj* [the connecting sacred objects] that link from Dhäliny to Dholtji. They were her mothers, carrying her in their own water.

KAYLEEN DJINGADJINGAWUY

MOKUY
Kayleen Djingdjingawuy Waṉambi, 2015

BAYWARRA BOY
Kayleen Djingadjingawuy, 2015

This is my son, Warren Jr., with two images of his grandfather. The face when he was alive, and the face he got on the night he passed away in 2014. Warren was his beloved grandson because he looks like him: his way of sitting, his movements, his *rumbal*, his face, his reactions... they look exactly the same. Same nose. They call my son *ma'mu* [grandfather] because his face is exactly like his grandfather.

The *djäri* represents the rainbow serpent, Witij. It represents his tribe and his *maḏayin* and his secret *gamunuŋgu*, which we picked up from the Internet. The lightning represents the lightning that the snake spits into the sky. Spreading that language to all the different lands, and he was telling himself: I'm here.

WARREN BALPATJI

When you see that Witij, rainbow snake, changing colour, that shows the *dhuyu rom* [the restricted law] of the Gurruwiwi people. The colours show the power of that man and his *rom*. Normally this kind of snake is just ordinary. But on a special occasion like a funeral or a circumcision ceremony we will paint that snake, showing its deep meanings and power.

Whenever you see the rainbow, you start crying. Your memory goes back to that land, to those people. It touches you. And you feel that old man, still there, close. *Balanda* probably only see a pretty rainbow. But it's meaningful. Yolŋu have strong feelings. From the eye contact with that rainbow it goes to your mind and to your heart. You start to worry straight away.

WARREN BALPATJI

DJÄRI FAMILY
Rayleen Warrinydhun Garmu, 2014

DJÄRI RELATIONS
Lillian Manybar Munungurr, 2014

The rainbow colours called *djäri* represent that old woman's mother. None of her sons would exist if not for their mother's mother. That rainbow-coloured background shows that. It holds them all together. The inter-linking hearts show they're missing her. Because she's gone.

MEREDITH BALANYDJARRK

Those girls call this rainbow *Djäri-gäthu*. They are *gäthu-wataŋu*. That means that their fathers are responsible for these colours, because this colour is *märi* for their fathers. Their fathers are *märi-wataŋu*. They put those special rainbow skirts on when my father passed away to perform special items at the funeral.

MEREDITH BALANYDJARRK

THE BLOOD OF JESUS
Rayleen Warrinydhun Garmu, 2013

THE ROOTS AND THE BRANCHES
Jessica Watmatja, 2014

These shots were taken at my father's funeral in 2013 at Yalakun. We wore red to represent the Dhaḻwaŋu flag and the blood of Jesus. The white is the brightness of God's glory.

Raelene put *djäpana* in the background because sunsets tell us to go back to the land through our minds and hearts and to think about family who've passed away.

MEREDITH BALANYDJARRK

This old woman, Dorothy Gudaltji, has passed away now. She's a Wangurri clan woman—you can tell here by her green-coloured dress.

Here she is surrounded by her grandchildren. Her *gutharra* from her daughters and her *gaminyarr* from her sons. She is the roots and they are the branches.

MEREDITH BALANYDJARRK

LARRPAN FAMILY
Jessica Ganambarr, 2014

DJUTARRA GIRLS
Selena Walmanytji, 2014

After you hear the first *wolma* thunder cloud, that signals that the wet season is coming, the clouds separate into different *wukun* [clouds].

KAYLEEN DJINGADJINGAWUY

These girls call themselves after a female spirit who lives in their homeland and cries for the bones of her ancestors. The background colours are *djäpana*, the colour of our sorrow. When you see the sunset anywhere in the world it connects us back to our land. And you can feel it. It touches your heart, because of the colours of Garrumarra [the octopus]. The stars represent our *märi*, Djurrpun Wirdiwu, that first morning star.

This photo is from a funeral where the girls performed a Christian *bungul* [dance] representing Garray [God] through all the different colours. I believe Garray gave us the colours. They give thanks to Garray with the colours.

MEREDITH BALANYDJARRK

When Hudson was young he called himself Elvis because he was a fan. When he sang *manikay* his voice sounded like Elvis's, so that's what people called him. Gurruwiwi people were the biggest fans of Elvis. For a while, when Hudson was living at East Arm Point near Darwin, he dressed like Elvis, in a jumpsuit. Those Gurruwiwi people liked to imagine Elvis was a member of their tribe, so looking at them here you can see these two men posed as Gurruwiwi brothers.

The water flowing behind is the Dhuwa moiety salt water, *garrkuluk raŋgurr*.

There's more here, too. The background sunset called *djäpana* shows that his wife was a Dhalwaŋu clan woman. She died long before Hudson. He missed her for many years. The cigarette in his mouth is another way of showing his longing for this lost Dhalwaŋu woman, because Dhalwaŋu people sing tobacco. It comes from their country. Deep inside. The songs tell us that.

The green colour of the rose leaves are for his *waku*, his sister's children, from the Wangurri people. Together, here, the red flowers and green leaves show the *märi-gutharra* relationship. That's the relationship that gives Dhalwaŋu people power and support.

We put them together because they are a team, or a family. It's all about that he's gone. His wife is gone. Finished. That represents everything gone.

That's his *gapu*, his clan waters. They sing that, *barkparkthun*, Dhuwa people singing with clapsticks. They sing the salt water and the fresh water. Both.

That *ŋarali'*, that cigarette, that is his *warwuyun*, what we call in English 'worry'. That's our Dhalwaŋu song, worrying for the *ŋarali'*. We sing that tobacco and dance it. And other Yirritja clans sing that *ŋarali'*, too, you're crying deeply for that *ŋarali'*... crying, crying.

WARREN BALPATJI

So we *warwuyun* through the *manikay*. Not only for *ŋarali'*. But that can open your mind back to the old people. It pulls everyone together connected through the *ŋarali'*, all those Yirritja clans who sing that tobacco, back through the *maḏayin*, through the *rom*.

PAUL GURRUMURUWUY

AFTERWORDS

Every time my phone rings, my stomach lurches. Even if I don't recognise the caller, I assume it's one of my Yolŋu family calling from a new number. They rarely call only to chat. They call because they need something. Or because they have something to tell me that I need to know. More often than not, it's bad news.

This week I received a call from one of my father's brother's sons. The second-to-last time we'd spoken I'd lent him a few hundred dollars so he could buy bits and pieces for a funeral ceremony. The last time, he'd told me he was in Adelaide with his nineteen-year-old son who was being treated for leukaemia. He was apologetic about not having paid me back; he'd had to give up his job at the Gapuwiyak store for at least three months so he could stay in Adelaide. Now his brother had died in Darwin. He'd been on dialysis and had gone drinking. Family were suspicious because he had seemed healthy, despite his kidney problems. (As usual, sorcery was suspected, though I heard only truncated versions of those stories later.) Lupurru told me he needed to fly to Darwin to organise the funeral. Again, he apologised for not being able to pay me back. I told him he should forget the debt.

The next day I got a call from my sister-in-law, Marrawaka'mirr. She was in Darwin for tests and likely needed chemo. With a little laugh, she said she'd had a heart attack while waiting for the results of the cancer tests. Now the chemo would have to wait until they'd taken a *bitja* of her heart. She's a couple of years older than me, in her late fifties. We talked for a while and I was struck by how upbeat she sounded. She told me that she was praying hard and had decided to refuse chemotherapy. I asked what had happened to the *bol'ŋu* stones with the special healing powers we'd collected together in her country, but she told me that she no longer had any; they'd long since disappeared, having taken themselves back home. She then asked for some money to do the Christmas shopping when she got out. Neither of us felt satisfied with the sixty dollars I transferred through my phone.

Each time I answer these calls I feel drawn into a world wider, deeper and somehow more alive than my university-focused life could ever be; a world of need, demand and generosity; a world that routinely confounds my expectations, and my capacities with its dynamics of relentless death and robust humour; a world in which, despite the impositions of colonial bureaucracies and assimilationist agendas, people remain stubbornly, often playfully, attentive to priorities and values that are of a distinctly different order to the insidious administrative agendas that shape my desk-bound days.

∎

JD Over the past twenty-five years, as I have collaborated on art and media projects in Gapuwiyak, I have been instructed—directly and indirectly—about the priorities of kinship and so been tested in my capacities to live it, and write about it, in ways that are adequate to the intensities, obligations, reciprocities, unruly eventfulness and oblique refusals that these familial bonds entail. I have welcomed this shared project of *yuṯa* anthropology as the means by which to refigure my own often awkward relationship with the discipline for which I've been trained. This is a discipline of audacious reach, slow-won insights, intrinsic limitations, but, nonetheless, as we have argued throughout *Phone & Spear*, significant participatory potential. However, in writing this book I have found myself wrenched by competing bursts of enthusiasm and apprehension; ambivalence is too mild a word to describe the lurching uncertainties that have repeatedly undermined my sense of purpose.

Countless times over the past decade, I have felt profoundly disheartened by what I cannot help but see as a deepening and irreversible social crisis unfolding in Gapuwiyak and its surrounding communities; despite the efforts of many, many brilliant and energetic artists, educators, musicians and political figures who have modelled forms of two-way living, Yolŋu society is undergoing a relentless transformation that I fear will have devastating consequences for current and future generations. The effects are incremental and hard to shake. I am not alone in thinking this; over the years that we have been working on this book two members of Miyarrka Media expressed their own worry that '*rom* is collapsing', meaning living in so-called remote communities is no longer a viable option; they mostly blame drugs, though they also identify other forms of pressure and distraction, including the phone.

And throughout the compilation of this text I have worried that our emphasis on the ancestral affordances of mobile phones has been at the expense of providing a bigger, and messier and much-harder-to-do-justice-to picture. I realise that one reason the texts in *Phone & Spear* have been assembled in fragments is because I don't know—none of us know—how to pull the pieces of the *yuṯa* world together into a coherent whole that includes not only mobile phones, but hip-hop and petrol and Coca-Cola and profits and welfare reform and casinos and mining and the fine art market and anthropology and renal dialysis and superannuation and boarding school and an education curriculum that fails to attract, let alone keep, the kids at school.

At such moments, the forms of connectedness we have celebrated in this book have seemed much too flimsy and fleeting; the sense of optimism expressed in these funny and poignant works seems extremely vulnerable in the face of relentless loss and change. Yet each time I lost heart and put the project aside, I found myself called back by the images themselves, repeatedly compelled by their tender beauty—and the ways that they produce small, yet transformative, moments of affirmation and possibility.

Such are the quiet and incremental effects of *dhäkay-ŋänhawuy rom*.
But what then?
Is it enough to locate solace and purpose in moments such as these?

.

JD   Last year, as we talked over a cup of coffee in Cairns, while the others headed out to hunt mangrove worms in the muddy tidal zone behind the house, I put these concerns directly to Gurrumuwuy. I told him that *balanda* already have a picture of places like Gapuwiyak from the media, and that they have the idea that the *yuṯa* generation is having a hard time finding a way forward, that they already have their own *bitja* of remote Aboriginal communities as sites of lawlessness, substance abuse and the breakdown of authority. I told him that I was worried that it might appear like we are deliberately ignoring this part of the picture by emphasising the social effects of using the phone 'in a good way'. The unsentimental certainty of his reply continues to shock me, even after all this time:

'I know what you mean, *gäthu*. I can see that the future is wrecked for the young people. I see that everywhere. I hope it doesn't come true.

'But for Yolŋu it doesn't matter how far you go, or how long you run, you are still in the foundation. You are walking with your identity, with your pattern, it's in your blood... It's all around, the pattern. Whether you are coming from *yapa* [your sister clans], or whether you are coming from *märi*. Your clan, your sacred objects and design, your *ŋändi*. Still there are connections. Links.

'It doesn't matter if you don't want to live with your *manikay* and *rom*, that *maḏayin* is still there. Your *dhulaŋ* [sacred designs] are still there. Your *bäpurru* still there. It is like a jigsaw puzzle. You might jump out, you might get lost with petrol sniffing or drugs, but that *rom* is always pulling you back in. Even through the phone.'

I nodded, then double-checked that my phone was recording.

As we were both well aware, this was a public declaration by the most senior member of our collective. His tone was convincing, his message compelling and well in keeping with the ways that other Yolŋu talk about the irreplaceable significance of country.

Yet to my ears, Gurrumuruwuy's certainty sounded disconcertingly optimistic. It seemed to fly in the face of all accruing evidence. (And here I could refer to the grim statistics that constitute the gap in life expectancies between Yolŋu and *balanda* in this country, or I could call to mind the backlog of bodies, young and middle-aged, waiting in the morgue for their turn to be buried in the clan lands in, and surrounding, Gapuwiyak. In another vein, I could refer to the mounting literature in anthropology that variously identifies the dynamics of structural violence, intergenerational trauma and social transformation that is resulting in Aboriginal people across remote parts of Australia becoming physically and ontologically dislocated from their ancestral homelands and traditions, with complex and socially destabilising effects.)

One could, of course, argue that Gurrumuruwuy has no other grounds from which to speak, quite literally. One could also say that without such stubborn certainty, nothing of substance remains for future generations; that without such ontological conviction, all is lost. There is no foundation, no *djalkiri*, no anchoring point in both time and space, no place from which to engage with the demands and possibilities of contemporary life, while actively recalling the past *and* imaginatively projecting oneself into the future.

But, of course, Gurrumuruwuy's point is that it is actually not simply a matter of belief: for him it is a matter of recognising and participating in the forceful agency of a self-assembling world; a more-than-human constellation of pattern and moral force that provides the template for its own renewal.

.

JD   Herein lies what I sometimes continue to experience as a profound irreconcilability in our expectations and outlooks, one that I first pointed towards in the Introduction, and that I think has been made evident at multiple moments in the text. It is in such moments that our shared project of *yuṯa* anthropology threatens to buckle, at least for me, as I feel a kind of moral responsibility arising from my own intellectual traditions and with that an urge to reach for explanation and analysis of a different order: to point to resilient colonial hierarchies of power and historically specific dynamics of social transformation that threaten to profoundly displace the ordered power of place and 'the old people', and so, in the process, to offer insights that might somehow pre-empt the wreckage to come, though I admit at this moment to having no conviction here with regard to my own capacity, or even old anthropology's potential as a discipline, making a lasting contribution in this respect, even if moments of recognition and 'shared feelings' of the kind we aim for here are achieved in the terms we hope for.

Melinda Hinkson is less equivocal in her call to action. She identifies '[t]wo vital tasks confronting anthropologists wherever precarity is apparent',

> (*a*) the documentation of the coexistence of differently ordered and contested modes of orientation to places and their interlinked forms of engagement with the world and (*b*) an accounting, where possible, of the historically contingent nature of newly emergent classificatory forms, or their absence, so as to reveal what is at stake in these transformations for the peoples with whom we work. *Adopting an interpretive framework that assumes openness and eschews hierarchy at the outset risks misrecognizing the multiple forms of constraint at play in any situation* [my emphasis].

Yuṯa anthropology, in its overt attempt to creatively mediate against precarity, hums along with the kind of anthropology advocated by Hinkson, even as it refuses to make the frictions arising from 'multiple forms of constraint' and 'contested modes of orientation' its primary orientation. The point, rather, as we have shown, and as I remind myself again now, is to claim vision (as part of a relational sensorium that prioritises a synaesthetic attention to the world) as socially generative—and so an essential aspect of Miyarrka Media's ongoing concern to invoke, nurture and renew an always-necessarily-shifting constellation of intergenerational and intercultural relationships. Our *yuṯa* anthropology recognises ways of seeing as cultural, historically contingent and yet nonetheless still potentially generative of new forms of relationship. The whole point of this book has been to demonstrate that it is possible to see past gaps, dissonance and dislocation through deliberate acts of showing, seeing, recalling and envisioning. Rupture, difference and disarray are not being overlooked—this is all too easy to perceive (especially for *balanda*). Rather, active seeing and receptive feeling is the *djäma* that matters here. The pleasures and satisfactions—as Guruṉulmiwuy told us right at the start—lies in the active process of finding and seeing connections that emerge from beneath a surface logics of appearance.

·

PG   Like I said, the Yolŋu world is like a jigsaw puzzle. Everything fits together. It doesn't matter how long you run, how far you drift. The *wäŋa* itself will pull you back. *Gurruṯu*, your family connections, will pull you back. That is the picture I'm giving out.

For *balanda*, we want you to see this too. To feel what we are sharing with you. Somehow. There are many layers in our Yolŋu world, many things that you will never be able see, or hear, or know, and I realise that it can be hard for you to understand everything that we have been telling and showing you here. That's why we try with this *yuṯa* anthropology to give you a taste of *dhäkay-ŋänhawuy rom*.

Everywhere you look these days, everyone is sitting with phones in our pockets and satellites overhead. Yolŋu and *balanda*. We can connect. We can learn from each other. We can share life. Why not?

JD   *Why not?* In an attempt to draw this text to a close, I once again return to the images and reflect on the ways they have reshaped my own appreciation of the power of ancestral homelands as they continue to shape the push-and-pull of Yolŋu life. What this book has charted are 'inside' places that satellites and GPS can never map; places that exist and flourish in the hearts and minds of kin who arrange themselves to manifest this patterned existence; sites inscribed in *muḻkurr* and *ŋayaŋu* that provide an experience of emplaced belonging and becoming-in-relationship that exert an urgent and yet stabilising force, even if one has never actually visited particular sites 'in the flesh'.

As I hope is clear by now, this is not intended as a testament to the mobile phone as a locative technology in any simple sense. If Gurrumuruwuy's certainty is located in the power of the *wäŋa* itself, it is a certainty affirmed through incremental moments of becoming-in-relationship to kin of many kinds, kin living in disparate places—in cities, homelands, in boarding schools and jails, in interstate training facilities and those who reside in spirit in forests and bushlands of the region—giving rise to experiences that accrue in affective traces of memory and recognition, that rise and settle on a *ŋayaŋu* through a lifetime of *dhäkay-ŋänhawuy rom*.

Recognition in this case is not simply an act of acknowledgement bestowed by one person or group upon another when categorical expectations are met. It is the product of a two-way process: the result of a social transaction instigated by acts of showing by someone or, in this case, entire families, who by entering the field of visibility are deliberately making themselves a public figure inciting response from the viewer. In this figuration connection is always ongoing and dynamic, shifting scales and orientation according to the context. Relational worlds like those that matter to Yolŋu are always taking shape. Acts of separation are therefore integral to the ongoing work of finding, forging and recognising connection anew.

If the phone has demonstrated the immanent relationality of the digital world in this book, what these photo collages and their accompanying stories of phones and spears and family make clear is that Yolŋu, like so many other social groups, are using the technology to reinscribe priorities and perspectives and so renew the Yolŋu world as distinctive and resilient. Even as they actively participate in the creation of a global world of digital connection, they resolutely refuse a call to assimilation, *jumping through the phone* and *bringing back* new materials for world-making, to insist on the durable vitality of a world structured by a bounded and differentiated set of values and social expectations.

And so this book puts out its call for a greater recognition of exactly this. At the very least my co-authors would hope that readers might now recognise that even when Yolŋu take up the technologies, the beats, the images and the consumer paraphernalia of a globalising world, Yolŋu should not be automatically seen to be assimilating into a global homogeneity. Look again. They are finding their own dances, their own style, their own *gakal*. Therein lies life.

·

JD Worlds of pattern are only possible if the pieces that make them up remain in motion and if those who seek them out remain open and alert to the shape of the next encounter, and the play of call-and-response it puts in motion, the associative resonances that come from seeing-as-if one thing is another. Vision Yolŋu-style means that each person gets to look out from where they are to see the world and locate themselves in shifting and always emergent patterns of relationship *yothu-yindi*, *märi-gutharra*, Yolŋu-*balanda*. Therein lies the liveliness, the grounds of continuity *and* possibility: a dynamic of social aesthetics capable of affirming foundational sacred depths *and* outward openings, depending on the patterns of association that get pieced together to make life as moments of coalescence, one *bitja* after another.

This Yolŋu mode of seeing is given a specific force and direction as *dhäkay-ŋänhawuy rom* is adapted to the intercultural work of relationship-making. Instead of relying on the moral force of country and the emplaced constellations of responsibility and connection embedded within it, the book seeks to activate and transmit affect and understandings stirred from inside Yolŋu hearts so that this might become palpable to others, moving beyond the pages in which it has been embedded, to stir the hearts and minds of readers, before settling down as a kind of accrued capacity to open and participate in expanding and interconnected worlds of relationship. (Though I would note that our collective expectations of the efficacy of this book in the terms we have outlined are cautious; we are curious rather than wildly optimistic about the reception of this work.)

Nonetheless, as we have shown, the mediated experiences of the kind we describe in this book are the means by which one participates in the shaping and reshaping of the world. It is this practised capacity to mediate connection (and so, necessarily, also deliberately enact decisive moments of disconnection and separation) in located bodies open to, and transformed by, relationships that my Yolŋu colleagues offer up as a form of a knowledge that can be of value to others, even as they undertake their own urgent, imaginative work of *seeing past difference and separation* as it manifests between the generations now growing up in troubled communities, drawing on the cheeky vitality of the new to remake an ancestrally ordered world that now co-exists and interacts with the relentless demands, distractions and opportunities of other worlds, now ever-more close to hand.

ACKNOWLEDGEMENTS

Assembling this book has been a decade-long labour of love. It would have been impossible without the help of family and friends.

We acknowledge the Dhaḻwaŋu *mala* and the Marraŋu *mala* together with other family, including Fiona Yangathu, Micky Dhambarra, Alison Gaḏayurr, Jessica Muthanhdhani, Trudie Garrumara, Gwenda Minganawuy, Sebastian Warruŋu, Katrina Dharraganmartji, Carmen Ḻirrayunmarrtja, Lindsay Ḻopurru, Joyce Walikur, George Ḻuḻparr Alfred Yaŋipuy, Carol Räminy, Andrew Banambi 2, Angeline Merrkiyawuy, Shadrick Dhawa, Georgina Warrangu, Renelle Barraḏakanbuy, Curtis Dhambali Wunuŋmurra, Mike Yamitjawuy Wunuŋmurra, David Wäpit Munuŋgurr, Lynne Wunuŋmurra, Shannadom Mayalmuṉu, Shirley Nirrpuranydji, Susan Marrawaka'mirr, Davis Marrawuŋgu, Dorothy Bamundurruwuy Dorothy Dhäparrawuy, Rowena Laypu, Samantha Yawulwuy, Natasha Ṉumbagawuy, Jacko Yipula, Antonio Daypulu, Alicia Burns, Gary Burns, Xena Waṉambi, Wesley Bandipandi, Helen Wilinydja, Joseph Yambaḻpurra, Richard Bulupal, Rose Waṉambi, Ṉuŋapan 1, Johnny Djeḻiwuy, Alfred Galaṉarawuy 2, Sharon and Alfred Wunuŋmurra and David Mackenzie. We acknowledge the generous contributions of all the artists and families who gave image permissions of their family and lost loved ones with future generations in mind. Cynthia Walaṉḏika and Dennis Rräŋa provided additional research. Gäwura Waṉambi kindly consulted on the final manuscript. *Marrkapmirr mala* [dear ones].

Gapuwiyak Culture and Arts Aboriginal Corporation has been a home for Miyarrka Media from its inception; we gratefully acknowledge all the Yolŋu directors and staff over the years, and especially managers Silke Roth and Trevor van Weeren. We thank the *Gapuwiyak Calling* exhibition teams at the University of Queensland Anthropology Museum Charla Strelan, Camella Harḏjo, Kiri Chan, Jane Willcock and Diana Young; Ruth Cohen and Dominic Davis at the American Museum of Natural History. Thanks also to Kerim Friedman and Gabriele de Seta for hosting our work in Taiwan for the Sensefield exhibition; and Vanessa Bartlett and Jill Bennett for commissioning the interactive touchscreen, *Warwuyun*, for the Group Therapy exhibition at UNSW Galleries. Special thanks to Oliver Warrwada Lanzenberg for cinematography on *Ringtone*. These collaborations all shaped this book.

Melinda Hinkson, Faye Ginsburg, Diana Young, Josh Bell, Haidy Geismar, Chris Wright, Fred Myers, Victoria Baskin Coffey, Michael Christie and Evan Wyatt have been exceptional friends to this project throughout its many iterations. Thank you. Nick Walton-Healey and Ton Otto provided incisive readings at crucial moments. We are in your debt. Jen Laylor offered much-needed legal advice. Thanks so much. Warm thanks also to Howard Morphy, Frances Morphy, Jessica De Largy Healy, Lucas Bessire, Juan Francisco Salazar, Steve Feld, Heather Horst, David Howes, Jacqueline Hazen, Cathy Greenhaugh, Christian Suhr, Andrew Irving, John Moran, Heather Swanson, Annette Markham, John von Sturmer, Jovan Maud, Richard Sherwin, Kirin Narayan, Ken George, Anna Tsing, Lisa Stefanoff, Jane Lydon, Deb Fisher, Suzanne Gibson, Mel Flanagan, Rhonda Black, Alison Leitch, Jennifer Biddle, Kym Druitt, Tony Dowmunt, Joseph Bell, Wade Jaffery, Nola Alloway, Stewart Lockie, Lars Skalman, Matthew Gingold and Jos Diaz Contreras. Will Owen, you are much missed. Jane Sloan, you are a remarkable editor and friend.

Sarah Kember, Adriana Cloud and Michelle Lo at Goldsmiths Press—thank you for taking up our little book with such enthusiasm. Santiago Carrasquilla and Eugene Lee at Art Camp—you lent your own *gakal*, *muḻkurr* and *ŋayaŋu* to the mix. How did we get so lucky?

Marrkapmirr mala.

Finally, we gratefully acknowledge funding support from Australian Research Council grants DP0877085 and FT110100587, UNSW Art and Design, Arts NT, The Cairns Institute and the College of Arts, Society and Education, James Cook University.

IMAGE CREDITS

MIYARRKA MEDIA
Simeon Rigamawuy
  Wunuŋmurra
Jennifer Deger
2019

PICTURED TOP LEFT,
CLOCKWISE
James Ganambarr
Meredith Balanydjarrk
Enid Guruŋulmiwuy
Warren Balpatji
Jennifer Deger
Paul Gurrumuruwuy
Kayleen Djingadjingawuy

WARRAGA
Santiago Carrasquilla
2017

LOCATION
Barge Landing Road,
  Gapuwiyak

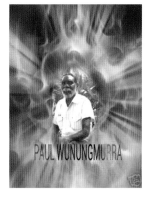

DHALWAŊU FIRE
Kayleen Djingadjingawuy
Waŋambi 2016

PICTURED
Paul Gurrumuruwuy
  Wunuŋmurra

DHALWAŊU FIRE 2
Kayleen Djingadjingawuy
Waŋambi Santiago
Carrasquilla 2017

PICTURED
Paul Gurrumuruwuy
  Wunuŋmurra

LOCATION
First Creek, Barge Landing
  Road, Gapuwiyak

LIKE HONEY
FROM HEAVEN
Simeon Rigamawuy
  Wunuŋmurra
2010

PICTURED TOP LEFT,
CLOCKWISE
Zacharia Djawilawuy
  Ganambarr
Paul Gurrumuruwuy
  Wunuŋmurra
Mathuis Wamuliyi Ganambarr
Katrina Dharraganmarttji
  Wunuŋmurra
Carman Lirunmartji
  Wunuŋmurra and Rickisha
  Dhapunali Munungurr
Fiona Yangathu Waŋambi

GUKU
Kayleen Djingadjingawuy
  Wanambi
2015

PICTURED TOP LEFT,
CLOCKWISE
Samuel Waliyinga Wanambi
Jodie Wanambi
Besma Dhaparrawuy
  Wanambi 2
Tasha Wanambi
Pryda Wunuŋmurra
Marsha Lurruwuy Marrawili
Charmaine Marrwungu
Melanie Marrawili
Jessica Wunuŋmurra
Madukan representing the
  spirit of the Yolŋu who
  passed away
Alice Yanananyŋu Wanambi
Janet Waymadiwuy
  Baird Wanambi 2
Spring Water Mirrany
  Gapu Wartwartunga
Kitora Bayini Wunuŋmurra

EVERYTHING IS HERE
Kayleen Djingadjingawuy
Wanambi 2017

PICTURED TOP LEFT,
CLOCKWISE
Terry Mamali Wunuŋmurra
Richard Bulupal Wunuŋmurra
Joyce Walikur Wunuŋmurra
Paul Gurrumuruwuy
  Wunuŋmurra

GROWING UP THE SAME
Renelle Barrandakanbuy
  Wunuŋmurra
2013

PICTURED
Renelle Barrandakanbuy
  Wunuŋmurra

SHARK BOYS
Simeon Rigamawuy
  Wunuŋmurra
2014

PICTURED LEFT TO RIGHT
Mathuis Madadbuma
  Ganambarr
Zachariah Djawalawuy
  Ganambarr

ŊURRUWUTTHUN,
EYE OF THE EAGLE
Kayleen Djingadjingawuy
  Wanambi
2017

PICTURED
Bulupal 2 Ngurruwuthun

WURRUMBA
Mandy Mandhamawuy
  Munyarryun
2014

PICTURED
Warren Balpatji Gurruwiwi

BÄRU
Kayleen Djingadjingawuy
  Wanambi
2015

PICTURED
Michael Yawundjur

FOOTY STARS
Renelle Barradakanbuy
  Wunuŋmurra
2013

PICTURED LEFT TO RIGHT
Gordon Mayathalaŋ
  Garawirrtja
Shadrick Dhawa Wunuŋmurra

SMM_JBW
Rowena Laypu Wunuŋmurra
2008

PICTURED LEFT TO RIGHT
Susan Marrawaka'mirr
Jennifer Deger

RED FLAG BOY
Simeon Rigamawuy
  Wunuŋmurra
2009

PICTURED
Wayne Guywuru Wunuŋmurra

MÄRI IS OUR BACKBONE
Kayleen Djingadjingawuy
  Wanambi
2015

PICTURED
Renelle Barrandakanbuy
  Wunuŋmurra
Kayleen Djingadjingawuy
  Wanambi
Paul Gurrumuruwuy
  Wunuŋmurra
Enid Guruŋulmiwuy
  Wunuŋmurra

GUMATJ FIRE
Jessica Ganambarr
2014

PICTURED LEFT TO RIGHT
Roslyn Bananaki Yunupingu
Janelle Gunanu Yunupingu
Steve Djati Yunupingu
Susan Watanynga Ganambarr
Selena Walmanytji Yunupingu
Jacqueline Wanguwuy
  Yunupingu

FIRST CREEK
Santiago Carrasquilla
2017

LOCATION
Barge Landing Road,
  Gapuwiyak

DHÄWU GA MANIKAY
Simeon Rigamawuy
  Wunuŋmurra
2015

PICTURED
Deven Mutjmi Ganambarr

COCONUT
Rowena Laypu Wunungmurra
2008

PICTURED
Alan Bäŋgana Wunuŋmurra

RINGTONE
Miyarrka Media
Video Still
2016

RINGTONE
Miyarrka Media
Video Still
2016

RINGTONE
Miyarrka Media
Video Still
2016

RINGTONE
Miyarrka Media
Video Still
2016

RINGTONE
Miyarrka Media
Video Still
2016

RINGTONE
Miyarrka Media
Video Still
2016

WILDFREE BOYS
Video Stills, MPEG-4
2010

WHAT A FEELING
Sherrie Munyaryun
Video Stills
2010

PICTURED
Jennifer Wunungmurra
Sylvia Retjarr
Dorothy Guyula
Rose Guyula
Helen Guyula

GOMU BOYS
Video Stills, MP4
2009

PICTURED
Yipuma Marrkula
Justin Nguyulngurra Guyula
Darren Mubulu Dhamarrantji
Djarrngani Guyula

BITJA DJÄMA
Santiago Carrasquilla
2017

PICTURED
Mayalmuŋgu Munungurr

BITJA DJÄMA
Santiago Carrasquilla
2017

PICTURED
Bambat Ganambarr

DJALKIRI,
OUR FOUNDATION
Simeon Rigamawuy
   Wunuŋmurra
2016

PICTURED
Richard Bulupal Wunuŋmurra
Terry Mamali Wunuŋmurra
Terry Ngutapuy Wunuŋmurra
Paul Gurrumuruwuy
   Wunuŋmurra

WURRAY HONEY HUNTER
Kayleen Djingadjingawuy
   Waṉambi
2016

WAṈAMBI FAMILY LOVE
Kayleen Djingadjingawuy
   Waṉambi
2015

PICTURED TOP LEFT,
CLOCKWISE
Alfred Galaṉarawuy Waṉambi
Joey Gulurung Waṉambi
Matthew Larmburr Waṉambi
Marcus Murmay Waṉambi
Rose Dhungurrawuy Waṉambi
Rebecca Mayamungu
   Waṉambi
Wayunga Waṉambi
Mikey Ngatjalal Waṉambi
Jacob Burrukuwuy Waṉambi
Djindirri Waṉambi
Dylan Dharatha Waṉambi
Roslyn Dhalapuray Waṉambi

CENTRE
Peter Wäpit Waṉambi

TWO WAṈAMBI BOYS
Kayleen Djingadjingawuy
   Waṉambi
2015

PICTURED LEFT TO RIGHT
Sebastian Geymul Waṉambi
Murphy Djambala Waṉambi

MY WAṈAMBI FAMILY
Kayleen Djingadjingawuy
   Waṉambi
2016

BAIRD FAMILY
Kayleen Djingadjingawuy
   Waṉambi
2015

PICTURED TOP LEFT,
CLOCKWISE
Belisha Gulwulyun
   Waṉambi Baird
Rodney Bikingu
   Waṉambi Baird
Janet Waymadiwuy
   Waṉambi Baird
Kayma Gardathun
   Dhamarandji
Shanadom Mayamungu
   Mununurr
Jacob Yirriyirr Waṉambi Baird
John-John Waṉambi Baird
Mishek Warrungu
   Wunuŋmurra 2
Unidentified
Jason Guyilirri Baird
Aaron Djambathun Baird
Clarence Rowu Baird

CENTRE
Bilin Waṉambi
Richard B. Wunuŋmurra
Richard Nginnginbuy
Waṉambi Baird

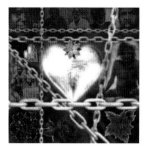

DESCENDANTS
OF DJALANDJAL
Kayleen Djingadjingawuy
Waṉambi
2015

PICTURED TOP LEFT,
CLOCKWISE
Ruth Bayni Wunuŋmurra
Joyce Waḻikur Wunuŋmurra
Paul Gurrumuruwuy
Wunuŋmurra
Terry Mamali Wunuŋmurra
Richard Bulupal Wunuŋmurra
Margaret Mary
Marlumbu Waṉambi
Mark Guywurru Wunuŋmurra

LUKU ṈALAPALMIRR
[THE FOOTSTEPS OF
THE OLD PEOPLE]
Mandy Mandhamawuy
Munyarryun
Santiago Carrasquilla
2017

PICTURED LEFT TO RIGHT
Paul Gurrumuruwuy
Wunuŋmurra
Mandy Mandhamawuy
Munyarryun

BROTHERS 4LIFE
Kayleen Djingadjingawuy
Waṉambi 2014

PICTURED TOP LEFT,
CLOCKWISE
Terry Malmaliny Wunuŋmurra
Richard Bulupal Wunuŋmurra
and Alyra Djuluwa Waṉambi
Terry Ngutapuy Wunuŋmurra
and Terry Malmaliny
Wunuŋmurra
Paul Gurrumuruwuy
Wunuŋmurra

ṈAYAṈU, MY DEEP
FEELINGS AS A
DHAḺWAṈU MAN
Mandy Mandhamawuy
Munyarryun
2014

PICTURED
Paul Gurrumuruwuy
Wunuŋmurra

DJINGADJINGAWUY
Kayleen Djingadjingawuy
Waṉambi
2016

PICTURED
Kayleen Djingadjingawuy
Waṉambi

LUKUWURRṈU
Mandy Mandhamawuy
Munyarryun
2014

PICTURED
Meredith Balanydjarrk
Wunuŋmurra

BALAWUKU GIRL
Jessica Ganambarr
2015

PICTURED
Katrina Dharraganmarttji
    Wununmurra

2_BROTHAZ_ARGUING
Jason Marpangar
    Dhamarrandji (Subtitles
    by Miyarrka Media)
Video Stills
2009

LONELY NYIKNYIK
Tristian Wathangani
    Munyarryun
Video Stills
2010

DHALATJ BIK
Celina Walmandji Yunupingu
2013

PICTURED
Wulula Munyarryun

DJÄPANA
Kayleen Djingadjingawuy
2015

PICTURED
Renelle Barradakanpuy
    Wununmurra

MAN'JTARR
[FLOATING LEAF]
Rowena Laypu Wununmurra
2011

PICTURED TOP LEFT,
CLOCKWISE
Alan Bängana Wununmurra
Rowena Lay'pu Wununmurra
    and Samantha Yawulwuy
    Wununmurra
Natasha Ngabagawuy
    Wununmurra
Jacko Yipula Wununmurra

CENTRE
Susan Marrawaka'mirr
    Marrawungu
Alan Bängana

WÄNANURA
[THE PROMISED LAND]
Artist Unidentified
2013

PICTURED
Joe Ngulundurowuy
    Garawirrtja
Nimatja Ganambarr

NEVER FORGOTTEN
Kayleen Djingadjingawuy
   Waṉambi
2015

PICTURED
Margaret Mary
Marlumbu Waṉambi

MOKUY
Kayleen Djingdjingawuy
   Waṉambi
2015

PICTURED
Don Garrala Gurruwiwi
Warren Jr Gurruwiwi
Don Garrala Gurruwiwi

DJÄRI FAMILY
Rayleen Warrinydhun Garmu
2014

PICTURED
Susan Watanyga Ganambarr
Nancy Yangulukbuy
   Ganambarr
Johnny Galmata Ganambarr
Jeffery Bortj Ganambarr
Jimmy Djawandjawan
   Ganambarr
Djirrmurrmurr Ganambarr
Dorothy Gudaltji Muyarryun
Wilson Guluwu Ganambarr

MINY'TJI OF THE ṈARRPIYA
Kayleen Djingadjingawuy
   Waṉambi
2015

PICTURED
Fiona Yangathu

BAYWARRA BOY
Kayleen Djingadjingawuy
Waṉambi 2015

PICTURED
Warren Watjapi 2 Gurruwiwl

DJÄRI RELATIONS
Lillian Manybar Munungurr
2014

PICTURED, LEFT TO RIGHT
Lillian Manybar Munuṉurr
Matal Munuṉurr
Sheree Munuṉurr
Ngakuyru Munuṉurr
Keisha Gurruwiwi

THE BLOOD OF JESUS
Rayleen Warrinydhun Garmu
2013

PICTURED LEFT TO RIGHT
Raelene Garmu
Nita Padawada Garmu
Jacqueline Wanguwuy
    Yunupingu
Meredith Balanydjarrk
    Wunuŋmurra
Selena Walmantj Yunupingu
Katrina Dharraganmarttji
Roslyn Bananaki Yunupingu
Janelle Gananu Yunupingu

LARRPAN FAMILY
Jessica Ganambarr
2014

PICTURED
Jim Djawanydjamany
    Ganambarr
Meredith Dhaypila Dhurrkay
Rhonda Dilmitjpiwuy
Vernon Rinyirrpum
Kathy Waritjawuy
Leon Ganngarrwuy
Simone Rrumbu
Kiara Gewu

TWO GURRUWIWI
BROTHERS
Mandy Mandhamawuy
    Munyarryun
2014

PICTURED
Hudson Djarwirr Gurruwiwi
Elvis Presley

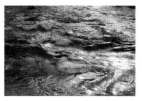

GAPU
Santiago Carrasquilla
2017

LOCATION
Barge Landing Road,
    Gapuwiyak

THE ROOTS AND
THE BRANCHES
Jessica Watmatja
2014

PICTURED
Dorothy Gudaltji with family

DJUTARRA GIRLS
Selena Walmanytji
2014

PICTURED
Jim Djawanydjamany
    Ganambarr
Meredith Dhaypila Dhurrkay
Rhonda Dilmitjpiwuy
Vernon Rinyirrpum
Kathy Waritjawuy
Leon Ganngarrwuy
Simone Rrumbu
Kiara Gewu

DJÄPANA
Santiago Carrasquilla
2017

LOCATION
Barge Landing Road,
    Gapuwiyak

NOTES

p.xxvi *From multiple sources;* see Zorc (1995) and Lowe (2014).

p.1 *Sacred patterns and our identity:* Yolŋu have a complex, patterned system of land and sea ownership that this book does not explicitly delve into, but which profoundly underpins the patterned sociality and relational ways of seeing that we describe. See Morphy and Morphy for an excellent account of these patterns as they manifest in clan-based kinship structures and everyday life practices that entail 'following ancestral patterns in the landscape' (2006:69).

p.10 *World-making devices:* Beginning with the publication of Horst and Miller's (2006) study of cell phones in Jamaica, the anthropological literature has offered numerous ethnographic case studies that show how these technologies can be enthusiastically taken up and embedded in local social contexts, often being used in ways that are 'non-standard' ways or 'purposely (re)configured' to serve local interests. As Vokes (2016) notes, until recently most anthropological studies have tended to demonstrate how the phone could support pre-existing social practices and values, enabling social reproduction, rather than serving as an agent of change. For other approaches to the social significance of mobile phones, see Doron and Jeffery (2013); Telban and Vávrová (2014); Grace (2014); Goggin and Hjorth (2014); Vokes and Pype (2016); Archambault (2017); Bell and Kuipers (2018). In the Australian Aboriginal context see Kral (2012, 2014); Vaarzon-Morel (2014); and Blakeman (2015). Vaarzon-Morel argues that mobile phones are only the most recent devices in a history of new technologies producing what she identifies as both 'integrative and disjunctive effects' in remote Aboriginal communities that includes the two-way radio and landline phones (2014:240).

p.11 *Yuṯa is exciting:* Innovation in Yolŋu art, performance and media is nothing new. As Marcia Langton has argued, innovations in Aboriginal art production point to 'a process of incorporating the non-Aboriginal world into the Aboriginal worldview or cosmology, to lessen the pressure for Aboriginal people to become incorporated or assimilated into the global worldview' (1994:90). In recent years there have many been remarkable figures in the music sphere who have demonstrated the Yolŋu genius for joining things together while refusing pressures to assimilate. In the sphere of music these include the late Gurrumul Yunupingu's sweet-voiced gospel, Baker Boy's bilingual hip-hop, and the *Djuki Mala*'s exuberant remix dance. The list of visual artists is too long to list here, but see Gapuwiyak Culture and Arts (www.gapuwiyak.com.au/); Buku-Larrŋgay Mulka Centre in Yirrkala; and the Mukla Project's work with media in Yirrkala (https://yirrkala. com/video-the-mulka-project/).

p.12 *Yolŋu collaborations:* The anthropological legacy in Arnhem Land is long. Anthropologists have worked in close, often collaborative, relationships with Yolŋu since the 1920s. See Warner (1969 [1937]); Williams (1986); Morphy (1991); McIntosh (2015); Keen (1994); Deger (2006); Tamisari (2005, 2016); De Largy Healy (2013), to name only a few. Yolŋu also have a long and important history of filmic collaborations in ethnographic, documentary and feature films. See Murray and Collins (2004) and de Heer and Djigirr (2006); see also Deveson's (2011) discussion of the Yirrkala Film Project. Given their openness to collaboration and emergent, contextually specific forms of knowledge production, Yolŋu have been at the forefront of an array of decolonising methodologies (Smith 2012) in a number of disciplines. See, for example,

Verran and Christie's STS approach (2014) and also the recent radical experiment in human geography of co-authoring with a Yolŋu Homeland that they credit as 'Country, Bawaka' in the list of authors including Country, Bawaka et al. (2016). In museum and material culture studies, the late Joe Gumbula from Elcho Island worked as a curator and advisor to collecting institutions, contributing in the process to the reshaping of anthropological practices and theories; Allen and Hamby (2011); while Don Gurruwiwi and his family co-curated with anthropologist John Carty a marvellous exhibition called *Yidaki: Didjeridu and the Sound of Australia* with the Museum of South Australia in 2017 (http://samyidaki.com.au/#).

p.13   *Rom*: This is difficult to translate into English. It is usually glossed as 'law', meaning broadly the values, structures and ways of life laid down by the ancestors. It can be used to refer to a code by which individuals live (people will say 'this is *my* rom' to talk about the specific values or ways of doing things that they claim as distinguishing aspects of their own life), but more generally the term refers to the foundational values embodied in, and materialised by, the *maḏayin* and the old people, or ancestors, who once held them in their care. There is a distinct and positively valued moral charge and authority to *rom*. Yolŋu characterise negative social changes in terms of people disregarding or abandoning *rom*. Clans and families within clans have their own particular *rom*. There is a mimetic aesthetic dimension of *rom* that is concerned with producing an ontologically generative field of sameness, though something of a different order to rote copying or repetition (see Deger 2006).

p.13   *Affect that moves between bodies, human and otherwise*: For other theorisations of the role of affect in contemporary Aboriginal society, see Jennifer Biddle's seminal work on Aboriginal art and intercultural relations in the central desert (2007, 2016); Fiona Magowan (2007) on Yolŋu women's song and crying; Bree Blakeman's (2015) account of Yolŋu economies of affect; and Deger (2016) on Yolŋu photography circulating as a distributed archive of affect that produces a spectral form of social 'thickening'. See also Elizabeth Edwards (2015) for an overaching discussion of photography and affect from anthropological perspectives.

p.15   *Two-way knowledges*: The two-way education curriculum development in Yirrkala based on forms of participatory research was just one notable example of the ways that Yolŋu metaphors are put into play to foreground the potentially dynamic interplay between Yolŋu and *balanda* epistemologies as productive and valuable. The late Raymatja Marika and Mandawuy Yunupingu were both extraordinary figures in this regard (not to mention Yunupingu's extraordinary contribution to Aboriginal rock music). See, for example, Marika, Ngurruwutthun and White (1992).

p.16   *Sensuous anthropology*: David Howes's recent article 'Multisensory Anthropology' (2019) offers a useful overview of the varying stakes in terms such as sensuous, multisensory and multimodal anthropology. Howes's abiding interest in the possibilities of 'sensory alterity' has made a major contribution to anthropology and the study of the senses. By stressing the need to attend to the formation of cultural and, by extension, gendered and class-based sensoria, Howes powerfully argues that the senses are 'made, not given' (2019:20). Interestingly, Howes turns to the anthropological literature on Arnhem Land in order to highlight the dynamics of what he calls '"audio-olfactory" and "visuo-olfactory" communication... at once chemical and aural-vibrational or visual"' (ibid. 23). Though not overtly theorised as such here (apart from Deger's use of the shorthand term 'synaesthetic' to gesture to the generative mutuality of the senses), there is a Yolŋu-honed intersensoriality vibrating through the pages of this book, a publication that might be described as an intercultural instruction manual for the senses.

p.16   *Evocative ethnography*: See Kathleen Stewart (2007) on writing affect; Haidy Geismar's work with photography, affect, presence and digital museum display in collaboration with a *Māori* artist and an interaction designer (2015b); Skoggard and Waterston (2015) more generally on the anthropology of affect and evocative ethnography; and Miyarrka Media's (2014, 2014a) earlier attempts at 'sharing feelings' through moving images and video screens. See also Tamisari (2005) on writing close to dance.

p.16   *Embedded aesthetics and relational accountability*: See Ginsburg (1994, 2018).

p.16   *Warpliri media*: Michaels (1993).

p.16   *Images, mutuality, regard*: See Deger (2006).

p.17   *Between art and anthropology*: This book does not overtly engage the ongoing disciplinary discussions regarding the relationship between art and anthropology, though see Marcus and Myers (1995); Schneider and Wright (2013); Grimshaw and Ravetz (2015); Geismar (2015a and 2015b); Cox, Irving and Wright (23016); and Bakke and Peterson (2017). It does, however, offer an explicit challenge to Tim Ingold's blunt assertion that the ethnographic obligation to context, particularity and 'rearwards' thinking makes it unsuitable for experiments between art and anthropology. Ingold writes, 'most attempts to combine art and anthropology, deliberately and self-consciously, have focused on ethnography as the glue that holds them together. These attempts have not, in my view, been wholly successful: they tend to lead both to bad art and bad ethnography'(2018:3). Beyond discussions focused around ideas of art, Deger's thinking in this book is energised by Kirin Narayan's (2016) depiction of 'everyday creativity' and Jean Burgess's (2009) discussions of 'vernacular creativity' in digital photography.

p.18   *Revelation and concealment*: As Fred Myers describes in a different context of Aboriginal art display, 'Concealment and control lie at the heart of an Indigenous performance that seeks to impress us with its value without accepting the dominance of those who view' (2014:281). In this respect, it is our considered acts of *not showing* and *not telling* that affirm *rom* and its enduring authority, the book providing *balanda* a glimpse of what Taussig describes as 'the skilled revelation of skilled concealment' (2016:455), gesturing to the twist of tension carried in each image, as the ever-present possibility of showing too much, or something that one does not have the rights to show at all, adding to the aesthetic force of each tender assemblage.

p.18   *Newness of new media*: See Gershon and Bell's (2013) recent edited collection of essays questioning the 'newness' of new media, including Deger (2013).

p.19   *Remix and remediation*: Bolter and Grusin (2000). See also Navas, Gallagher and Burrough (2015) for an introduction to the growing field of remix studies.

p.35   *The moving mind meets the moving body*: Taussig (2015:41).

p.36   *Tribes or clans?*: After some debate over terminology amongst an earlier generation of *balanda* anthropologists, the term clan is now generally used as a descriptor for the patrilineal descent groups through which Yolŋu society is structured and patterned. In this book, however, the terms tribes and clans have been used interchangeably, reflecting the fact that Yolŋu are more confortable with the term tribe because of their familiarity with English-language versions of the Bible.

p.41   *An increasingly digital world*: Miyarrka Media (2014b:3). The 3G network had been preceded by the CDMA network, which had been connected several years earlier and had enabled more basic talk and text functions.

p.41   *Balanda technologies*: Over the past two decades many scholars researching digital media in remote Indigenous communities in Australia have focused on the design and implementation of databases and other forms of digital archiving and delivery that operate in accordance with local epistemological and social imperatives (Christen 2005; Christie 2008; Gumbula, Corn and Mant 2013; Verran, Christie, Anbins-King, van Weeren and Yunupingu 2007; Corn and Gumbula 2003; Thorner and Dallwitz 2015). Kral (2010) identifies the ways that social media use amongst Indigenous youth cultures in Central Australia gives rise to new forms of literacy. See the edited collection of essays in *Cultural Studies Review* by Biddle and Stefanoff for a discussion of 'Indigenous aesthetics and intercultural cosmopolitanisms' (2015:100) that sit far closer to the *ethos* of this book. More recently, anthropological discussions of Indigenous media in Australia and elsewhere have turned to imaginaries of the future (Lempert 2018; Hennessy, Smith and Hogue 2018; Ginsburg 2018a).

p.41   *Each time the phone rings*: Miyarrka Media (2014).

p.42   *Rather than difference*: Audra Simpson's critique of anthropology as the presumptive voice of indigeneity underscores 'culture' as a category of colonisation: '"Culture" described the difference that was found in these places and marked the ontological end-game of each exchange: a difference that had been contained into neat, ethnically-defined territorial spaces that now needed to be made sense of, to be ordered, ranked, to be governed, to be possessed' (2007:67).

p.42   *Bark paintings*: See Morphy (1989, 1991, 2007) for a comprehensive overview of the emergence and significance of bark painting as a distinctive art form. Morphy's research and writing has been instrumental in facilitating the international recognition of the diversity, skill and sheer brilliance of Yolŋu artists and Yolŋu art forms. See also 'The art of Yirrkala crayon drawings – innovation, creativity and tradition,' in which Morphy describes another formal experiment in Yolŋu art arising from 'a synergistic relationship between the motivations of the anthropologist and the motivated engagement of the Yolngu' (2013:29). Many museums and galleries, incluing the National Museum of Australia, display images of significant works online along with narrative explanations provided by the artist for those interested in seeking out these often astonishingly beautiful and richly meaningful forms of *gamunuŋu*. See Pinchbeck (2018), *Noŋgirrŋa Marrawili: From my Heart and Mind*, the catalogue from an extradinary recent exhibition of bark painting, sculptures and work on paper that chimes deeply with the themes of this book.

p.52   *Waŋgany*: Frances Morphy (2008:128) underscores the goal of inclusive harmony in Yolŋu governance. As she writes, 'Ultimately a "good" leader is a person to whom other people will listen, and who can create and maintain consensus—a sense of *ŋayaŋu wanggany* "one feeling" or *mulkurr wanggany* "one mind"'. See Blakeman (2015:411) for a nuanced description of 'the normative ideal and primary value of ŋayaŋu-wanggany'.

p.55   *A politics of affirmation*: This term is borrowed from Rosi Braidotti (2010).

p.56   *Thinking through assemblages*: Tsing (2015:22–23).

p.62   *Shared anthropology*: The term 'shared anthropology' is most closely associated with the French ethnographc filmmaker Jean Rouch, who made films that asserted the generative, performative and downright exuberant possibilities of a collaborative anthropology. See, for example, Rouch and Feld (2004).

p.63   *Colour materialises relationships*: See Diana Young's seminal work on the materiality of colour (2006, 2011, 2018). As she writes, 'Colours constitute badges of identity and connect otherwise disparate categories of things... colours can transform things... Colours are also linked to emotional expression. Lastly in the phenomenon known as synaesthesia coloured mental imagery is linked with other senses, not just the visual – commonly sound, odour, and tactility' (2006:ibid).

p.77   *Structural violence*: Sociologist Johan Galtung (1969) coined this term to refer to the oppressive power of social institutions whereby they produce harm on people as they impose and perpetuate inequality such as poverty and racism. Structural violence enables an analytic position that approaches social suffering within a broader history of marginalisation and, in the case of Indigenous people, the ongoing imposition of colonial structures of governance, education and administration as informed by the normative social expectations of the settler society.

p.78   *Anticolonial struggle*: cf. Jennifer Biddle's (2016) situating of new and experimental Aboriginal artforms in Central Australia. It is worth emphasing also that the ways of seeing that drive this project arc not constituted in response to the colonial archive and its enduring, though by now much-criticised, visual tropes. See, for example, Langton's subtle analysis of Brook Andrew's 'enchantment of ethnographic photographs' (2014). See also Lydon (2005, 2014) on Aboriginal people's relationships with archival photographs beyond the art sphere.

p.78   *Affordances*: Media scholars use the term 'affordances' as a way to identify technologies for what they do or enable, rather than what they are. It is a relational approach to thinking about technological effects; a way of moving past technologically determinist assumptions that technologies impact societies and individuals—or, conversely, the idea that technologies are simply what humans create them to be. See, for example, Bucher and Helmond (2018).

p.79   *Two worlds*: See Frances Morphy's (2007) discussion of Yolŋu conceptualising themselves as living in 'two worlds' and the intercultural zone created by organisations such as the Laynha Homelands Association.

p.80   *Co-creativity*: See, for instance, the rhetoric of empowerment on the Blingee photo app site: 'Traditional photos are boring, and we thought you deserved much better than the same graphics and content with no personality used over and over again across the net... so we decided to put the power back in your hands, and give you simple to use tools to create your own masterpieces that express your own ideas, feelings, and emotions!' (https://blingee.com/about).

p.80   *The disappearance of place*: Taylor (2014:2).

p.81   *Co-creativity*: See Haviland (2017) for discussions of co-creativity and collaboration in a variety of contexts, including Aboriginal Australia.

p.86   *Lightning snake ringtone recording*: Canadian anthropologist and ethnomusicologist Peter Toner worked closely with Bäŋgana for several years during his own PhD research, producing a valuable archive and an analysis of clan *manikay* that highlights song poetry as a fundamental dimension of Yolŋu poetics and imagistic world-making (2001, 2003). The translation of the song on the following page is from Toner (2001:358–359), with the orthography and spelling amended for this publication by Gäwura Waṉambi.

p88   *Galka*: Though technology itself can be a vector of malicious magic by humans (*galka*), it does not provide access for the spirit world to communicate directly as described by Telban and Vávrová (2014) in New Guinea.

p.94   *Hiding*: Turkle (2011:1).

p.96   *Completely freaked her out*: See Miyarrka Media's film *Ringtone* (2014) for more stories of *galka*, SIM card swapping and *balanda* phone scams.

p.127   *Without accepting the dominance of those who view*: Myers (2014:281).

p.127   *The skilled revelation of skilled concealment*: Taussig (2016:455). Morphy elaborates these revelatory dynamics in Yolŋu in more 'traditional' art forms such as painting and sculpture (1991, 2003).

p.151   *Wangarr can be seen as a manifestation of the one true God*: Morphy (2003).

p.171 *2_Brothaz_Arguing*: A google search identified the original video as an episode of *Bewitched* (S3, E26: *Aunt Clara's Victoria Victory*. www.dailymotion.com/video/x2giyg3_ bewitched-s3-e26-aunt-clara-s-victoria-victory_fun).

p.182 *Yolŋu metaphors for learning*: Marika-Mununggiritj and Christie (1995:60). The article discusses key Yolŋu concepts identified in consultation with community elders at Yirrkala Community School as part of a program of Yolŋu curriculum development. '[W]e learn to recognise what we see in the environment and how it can help us.' Next, they introduce the expression ☆*undu-nhäma*. *Nhäma* translates pretty straightforwardly as 'to see'. *Lundu*, they explain, is more complex. It can refer to the creative journeys made by ancestors; it can also refer to the footsteps or gait of these people. If we understand *Lundu* as manifestation of shared characteristics or similarity across distance, then the final definition they offer also makes sense: 'a word for friend, or companion, someone who thinks and feels so close to your, they are almost like your reflection'. Marika-Mununggiritj states: 'First we must recognise what has gone before and know exactly how it fits within the whole web of meaning which makes Yolŋu life.' It is this act of reproduction, albeit in a modern guise, that has effects that far exceed what we might understand if we turned only to the Yolŋu dictionary for explanation, where *dhuḏakthun* translates as act, pretend, imitate, learn, or copy.' *Dhuḏakthun*, as Marika-Mununggiritj and Christie describe, 'has the effect of bringing our [Yolŋu] spiritual past *to life again* through our modern behaviour' (my italics). Marika-Mununggiritj and Christie (1995:60–61).

p.184 *Technological redemption*: Hinkson (2013:303).

p.185 *Let us love this distance*: Solnit (2005:31).

p.187 *More family photographs*: Deger (2015); Miyarrka Media (2011).

p.188 *A manifestation of ancestral power*: See, for example, Morphy (1989, 1991).

p.189 *Oh yes! Expression of discovery*: Charles Darwin University, Yolŋu Matha Dictionary (http://Yolŋudictionary.cdu.edu.au/).

p.196 *Artist unidentified*: Occasionally, we have been unable to identify the artist/ photographer. This did not particularly bother other members of Miyarrka Media who were less interested in who made the image than who and what it showed.

p.212 *Structural violence, intergenerational trauma, and social transformation*: See, for example, Lea, Kowal and Cowlishaw (2006); Altman and Hinkson (2010); Austin-Broos (2011); Sutton (2011); Povinelli (2016); Eickelkamp (2017); and a recent collection of essays in the special issue of *Oceania: Shifting Indigenous Australian Realities: Dispersal, Damage, and Resurgence*, edited by Hinkson and Vincent (2018).

p.213 *Recognition*: See Hinkson (2017b:90) on the failure of recognition: 'Recognition forecloses rather than opens possibilities for transformative interactions across cultural forms.'

p.213 *Wherever precarity is apparent*: Hinkson defines precarity as 'the ontological disembedding of people from distinctively place-based associations' (2017a:58).

GLOSSARY

B

balanda: European, white, non-Aboriginal, derived from 'Hollander'; Macassan-introduced word
bäpurru: clan, group, funeral.
barrkuwatj: separate, far apart
bäru: crocodile
bäyim: to buy, pay
biŋk: pink; can also be a Yolŋu term for balanda, or non-Aboriginal, woman
birrimbirr: spirit
bitja: photograph, film, video, picture
buŋgul: dance, ceremonial dance
buku-manapanmirr: joining or bringing things together

d

dhäkay-ŋänhawuy rom: the law of feeling; relationship through feeling
Dhalwaŋu: Yirritja clan
dharpa: tree, stick
dhäruk: speech, language, advice, message
dhay'yi: this
dhulaŋ: sacred designs
dhuwa: one of the two moieties of which the Yolŋu world is comprised, along with yirritja
djäl: what one is drawn close to through want, desire or love
djalkiri: foundation, foot
djäma: work
djambatj: 'one shot', good at (hunting, gathering, fishing), expert, quick, accurate
djarraṯawun': flash or light
djorra': book
djuŋaya: ceremonial manager and supervisor [see waku]
doturrk: heart

g

gaḏayka': stringybark tree
gakal: style
galka: sorcerer
galpu: spear thrower
gamunuŋgu: clay, ochre, paint, sacred design
ganydjarrmirr: powerful
gäthu: son or daughter from father or woman's brothers' children
gara: spear
guku: honey
gurruṯu: family, kin(ship)
gurtha: fire
gutharra: grandchild; reciprocal relationship is märi

l

luku: foot, root of a tree, foundation, anchor

m

maḏayin: secret, sacred
mäṉa: shark
manikay: song, clan song
manymak: good
maranydjalk: stingray
marrkap: expression of affection, love and gratitude
marrkapmirr mala: strong expression of affection, love and gratitude addressed to a group
märi: maternal grandmother, grand-uncle on mother's side; reciprocal relationship is gutharra
märi-gutharra: relationship of mother's mother between people or groups (märi-gutharra are pairs from different clan groups, but with common stories, totems, names and ceremonies)
matha: language, literally tongue
meyawa: frilled-neck lizard
miny'tji: colour, pattern
mirriny: beehive entrance
mori: father
mukul rumaru: mother-in-law (avoidance relationship)
muḻkurr: head, mind
mulmul: sea foam, lather, froth, suds, bubbles
munatha: sand, soil

ŋ

ŋändi: mother
ŋänitji: alcohol
ŋaraka: carapace, shell, handset, bone
ŋarali': cigarettes, tobacco
ŋarrpiya: octopus

ŋatha: food
ŋathi: maternal grandfather, granduncle
ŋayaŋu: heart, soul, sacred object

n   **nyumikiny:** small

r   **raki':** string, mobile phone
riŋgitj: a sacred place for specific people or groups of people
rirrakay: sound, noise, voice, mobile phone
rom: law, tradition, way of life
rrupiya: money; Macassan-introduced word
rumbal: body, tree trunk

w   **waku:** woman's children, man's sisters' children; these people are djuŋgaya for their mothers' clan business
walŋa: alive
wäŋa: land, home
waŋgany: one, united
warwuyun: active sorrow, worrying, pining (noun form: warwu)
wäwa: brother
wuŋili': image, photograph, shadow

y   **yä:** expression of discovery, spoken when making a connection
yawirriny': young or single men
yapa: sister
yiki: knife
yindipuy: large
yirritja: one of the two moieties of which the Yolŋu world is comprised, along with dhuwa
Yolŋu: Aboriginal person from northeast Arnhem region, Aboriginal person more generally, and by extension sometimes just person
yuṯa: new

REFERENCES

Allen, Lindy, and Louise Hamby. 2011. 'Pathways to Knowledge: Research, Agency and Power Relations in the Context of Collaborations Between Museums and Source Communities'. In *Unpacking the Collection: Networks of Material and Social Agency in the Museum*, 209–229. New York: Springer.

Altman, Jon, and Melinda Hinkson. 2010. *Culture Crisis: Anthropology and Politics in Aboriginal Australia*: UNSW Press.

Archambault, Julie Soleil. 2017. *Mobile Secrets: Youth, Intimacy, and the Politics of Pretense in Mozambique*. Chicago: University of Chicago Press.

Austin-Broos, Diane. 2011. *A Different Inequality: The Politics of Debate about Remote Aboriginal Australia*. Crows Nest, NSW: Allen & Unwin.

Bakke, Gretchen, and Marina Peterson. 2017. *Between Matter and Method: Encounters in Anthropology and Art*. London: Bloomsbury.

Bell, Joshua A., and Joel C. Kuipers, eds. 2018. *Linguistic and Material Intimacies of Cell Phones*. London: Routledge.

Biddle, Jennifer. 2007. *Breasts, Bodies, Canvas*. Sydney: UNSW Press.

Biddle, Jennifer. 2016. *Remote Avant-Garde: Aboriginal Art Under Occupation*. Durham, NC: Duke University Press.

Biddle, Jennifer, and Lisa Stefanoff. 2015. 'What Is Same but Different and Why Does It Matter?' *Cultural Studies Review* 21 (1):97–120.

Blakeman, Bree. 2015. 'Exploring the Role of Affect in Yolŋu Exchange'. *The Australian Journal of Anthropology* 26 (3):398–413.

Bolter, Jay David, and Richard Grusin. 2000. *Remediation: Understanding New Media*. Cambridge, MA: The MIT Press.

Braidotti, Rosi. 2010. 'On Putting the Active Back into Activism'. *New Formations* 68 (Spring):42–57.

Bucher, Taina, and Anne Helmond. 2018. 'The Affordances of Social Media Platforms'. In *The SAGE Handbook of Social Media*, edited by Jean Burgess, Thomas Poell and Alice Marwick, 233–253. London: Sage Publications.

Burgess, Jean. 2009. 'Remediating Vernacular Creativity: Photography and Cultural Citizenship in the Flickr Photo-Sharing Network'. In *Spaces of Vernacular Creativity: Rethinking the Cultural Economy*, edited by Tim Edensor, Deborah Leslie, Steve Millington and Norma M. Rantisi, 116–126. London and New York: Routledge.

Christen, Kimberly. 2005. 'Gone Digital: Aboriginal Remix in the Cultural Comments'. International Journal of Cultural Property 12:315–344.

Christie, Michael. 2008. 'Digital Tools and the Management of Australian Desert Aboriginal Knowledge'. In *Global Indigenous Media: Cultures, Practices and Politics*, edited by P. Wilson and M. Stewart, 270–286. Durham, NC: Duke University Press.

Corn, Aaron, and Neparrna Gumbula. 2003. '"Djiliwirri Ganha Dharranhana, Waŋa Limurruŋu": The Creative Foundations of a Yolŋu Popular Song'. *Australasian Music Research* 7:55–66.

Country, Bawaka, Sarah Wright, Sandie Suchet-Pearson, Kate Lloyd, Laklak Burarrwanga, Ritjilili Ganambarr, Merrkiyawuy Ganambarr-Stubbs, Banbapuy Ganambarr, Djawundil Maymuru and Jill Sweeney. 2016. 'Co-Becoming Bawaka: Towards a Relational Understanding of Place/Space'. *Progress in Human Geography* 40 (4):455–475.

Cox, Rupert, Andrew Irving and Christopher Wright, eds. 2016. *Beyond Text*. Manchester: Manchester University Press.

de Heer, Rolf, and Peter Djigirr. 2006. *Ten Canoes*. Palace Cinemas.

Deger, Jennifer. 2006. *Shimmering Screens: Making Media in an Aboriginal Community, Visible Evidence*. Minneapolis, MN: University of Minnesota Press.

Deger, Jennifer. 2008. 'Imprinting on the Heart: Photography and Contemporary Yolngu Mournings'.

Visual Anthropology 21 (4):292–309.

Deger, Jennifer. 2013. 'In-Between'. In *Anthropology and Art Practice*, edited by A. Schneider and C. Wright, 105–114. Oxford: Berg.

Deger, Jennifer. 2014. *Gapuwiyak Calling: Phone-Made Media from Arnhem Land*, edited by University of Queensland Anthropology Museum. Brisbane.

Deger, Jennifer. 2016. 'Thick Photography'. *Journal of Material Culture* 21 (1):111–132.

Deveson, Philippa. 2011. 'The Agency of the Subject: Yolngu Involvement in the Yirrkala Film Project'. *The Journal of Australian Studies* 35 (2):153–164.

Doron, Assa, and Robin Jeffrey. 2013. *The Great Indian Phone Book: How the Cheap Cell Phone Changes Business, Politics, and Daily Life*. Cambridge, MA: Harvard University Press.

Edwards, Elizabeth. 2015. 'Anthropology and Photography: A Long History of Knowledge and Affect'. *Photographies* 8 (3):235–252.

Eickelkamp, Ute. 2017. 'Finding Spirit: Ontological Monism in an Australian Aboriginal Desert World Today'. *HAU: Journal of Ethnographic Theory* 7 (1):235–264.

Feld, Steven (ed). 2003. *Ciné-Ethnography*. Minneapolis, MN: University of Minnesota Press.

Galtung, Johan. 1969. 'Violence, Peace, and Peace Research'. *Journal of Peace Research* 6 (3):167–191.

Geismar, Haidy. 2015a. 'Anthropology and Heritage Regimes'. *Annual Review of Anthropology* 44:71–85.

Geismar, Haidy. 2015b. 'Post-Photographic Presences, or How to Wear a Digital Cloak'. *Photographies* 8 (3):305–321.

Geismar, Haidy. 2015c. 'The Art of Anthropology: Questioning Contemporary Art in Ethnographic Display'. In *The International Handbooks of Museum Studies: Museum Theory*, edited by Andrea Witcomb and Kylie Message, 183–210. Chichester: John Wiley & Sons, Ltd.

Gershon, Illana, and Joshua Bell. 2013. 'Introduction: The Newness of New'. *Media, Culture, Theory and Critique* 54 (3):259–264.

Ginsburg, Faye. 1994. 'Embedded Aesthetics: Creating a Discursive Space for Indigenous Media'. *Cultural Anthropology* 9 (3):365–382.

Ginsburg, Faye. 2018. 'Decolonizing Documentary On-Screen and Off: Sensory Ethnography and the Aesthetics of Accountability'. *Film Quarterly* 72 (1):39–49.

Ginsburg, Faye. 2018a. 'The Indigenous Uncanny: Accounting for Ghosts in Recent Indigenous Australian Experimental Media'. *Visual Anthropology Review* 34 (1):67–76.

Goggin, Gerard, and Larissa Hjorth. 2014. 'Introduction: Mobile Media Research— State of the Art'. In *The Routledge Companion to Mobile Media*, edited by Gerard Goggin and Larissa Hjorth, 1–8. New York and Oxon: Routledge.

Grace, Helen. 2014. *Culture, Aesthetics and Affect in Ubiquitous Media: The Prosaic Image*. London and New York: Routledge.

Grimshaw, Anna, and Amanda Ravetz. 2015. 'The Ethnographic Turn – and After: A Critical Approach Towards the Realignment of Art and Anthropology'. *Social Anthropology* 23 (4):418–434.

Gumbula, Joseph, Aaron Corn and Julia Mant. 2013. 'Discovering the Earliest Shadows: A Yolŋu-Led Approach to Managing Community Access to Archived Cultural Resources'. In *Information Technology and Indigenous Communities*, edited by Lyndon Ormond-Parker, Aaron Corn, Cressida Fforde, Kazuko Obata and Sandy O'Sullivan, 197–206. Canberra: AIATIS Research.

Gurrumuruwuy, Paul, and Jennifer Deger. 2019. 'The Law of Feeling: Experiments in a Yolngu Museology'. In *The Routledge International Handbook of New Digital Practices in Galleries, Libraries, Archives,*

Museums and Heritage Sites, edited by
Hannah Lewi, Wally Smith, Steve Cooke
and Dirk vom Lehn. Oxford: Routledge.

Haviland, Maya. 2017. *Side by Side?
Community Art and the Challenge
of Co-Creativity*. New York
and Oxon: Routledge.

Healy, de Largy. 2013. 'Remediating
Sacred Imagery on Screens: Yolngu
Experiments with New Media
Technology'. In *Australian Aboriginal
Anthropology Today: Critical Perspectives
from Europe*. Paris: Musee du quai Branly.

Hennessy, Kate, Trudi Lynn Smith and
Tarah Hogue. 2018. 'ARCTICNOISE and
Broadcasting Futures: Geronimo Inutiq
Remixes the Igloolik Isuma Archive'.
Cultural Anthropology 2 (33):213–223.

Hinkson, Melinda. 2013. 'Back to the
Future: Warlpiri Encounters with
Drawings, Country and Others
in the Digital Age'. *Culture, Theory
and Critique* 54 (3):301–317.

Hinkson, Melinda. 2014. *Remembering
the Future: Warlpiri Life through
the Prism of Drawing*. Canberra:
Aboriginal Studies Press.

Hinkson, Melinda. 2017a. 'Precarious
Placemaking'. *Annual Review of
Anthropology* 46 (1):49–64.

Hinkson, Melinda. 2017b. 'Beyond
Assimilation and Refusal: A
Warlpiri Perspective on the Politics
of Recognition'. *Postcolonial
Studies* 20 (1):86–100.

Hinkson, Melinda, and Eve Vincent. 2018.
'Shifting Indigenous Australian
Realities: Dispersal, Damage,
and Resurgence: Introduction'.
Oceania 88 (3):240–253.

Horst, Heather, and Daniel Miller. 2005.
'From Kinship to Link-up Cell Phones
and Social Networking in Jamaica'.
Current Anthropology 46 (5):755–778.

Horst, Heather A., and Daniel Miller. 2006.
*The Cell Phone: An Anthropology of
Communication*. London: Bloomsbury.

Horst, Heather A., and Daniel Miller,
eds. 2012. *Digital Anthropology*.

London and New York: Berg.

Howes, David. 2019. 'Multisensory
Anthropology'. *Annual Review
of Anthropology* 48:17–28.

Ingold, Tim. 2013. *Making: Anthropology,
Archaeology, Art and Architecture*.
London: Routledge.

Ingold, Tim. 2018. 'Art and Anthropology
for a Living World'. Lecture in
series Prendre le parti des choses.
Publications hybrides sur les processus
de création l'École nationale supérieure
des Arts Décoratifs, 29 March 2018.

Keen, Ian. 1994. *Knowledge and Secrecy in
an Aboriginal Religion*. Melbourne:
Oxford University Press.

Kral, Inge. 2010. *Plugged In: Remote
Australian Indigenous Youth and Digital
Culture*. Canberra: CAPER, ANU.

Kral, Inge. 2012. *Talk, Text and
Technology: Literacy and Social
Practice in a Remote Indigenous
Community*. Bristol, Buffalo, NY and
Toronto: Multilingual Matters.

Kral, Inge. 2014. 'Shifting Perceptions,
Shifting Identities: Communication
Technologies and the Altered
Social, Cultural and Linguistic
Ecology in a Remote Indigenous
Context'. *The Australian Journal of
Anthropology* 25 (2):171–189.

Langton, Marcia. 1994. 'Aboriginal Art and
Film: The Politics of Representation'.
Race and Class 35 (4):89–106.

Langton, Marcia. 2014. 'Brook Andrew:
Ethical Portraits and Ghost-Scapes'.
*Art Journal, National Gallery of
Victoria* 48. www.ngv.vic.gov.au/
essay/brook-andrew-ethical-
portraits-and-ghost-scapes/.

Lea, Tess, Emma Kowal and Gillian
Cowlishaw, eds. 2006. *Moving
Anthropology: Critical Indigenous Studies*.
Darwin: Darwin University Press.

Lempert, William. 2018. 'Indigenous
Media Futures: An Introduction'.
Cultural Anthropology 33 (3):173–179.

Lowe, Beulah. 2014. *Yolŋu-English
Dictionary*. Darwin: ARDS inc.

Lydon, Jane. 2005. *Eye Contact: Photographing Indigenous Australians*. Durham, NC: Duke University Press.

Lydon, Jane. 2014. *Calling the Shots: Aboriginal Photographies*. Canberra: AIATSIS Press.

Magowan, Fiona. 2007. *Melodies of Mourning: Music and Emotion in Northern Australia*. Oxford: James Currey.

Marcus, George, and Fred R. Myers, eds. 1995. *The Traffic in Culture: Refiguring Art and Anthropology*. Berkeley, CA: University of California Press.

Marika, Raymattja, Dayngawa Ngurruwutthun and Leon White. 1992. 'Always Together, Yaka Gäna: Participatory Research at Yirrkala as Part of the Development of a Yolngu Education'. *Convergence* 25 (1):23–39.

Marika-Mununggiritj, Raymattja, and Michael Christie. 1995. 'Yolngu Metaphors for Learning'. *International Journal of the Sociology of Language* 113(1):59–62.

McIntosh, Ian. 2015. *Between Two Worlds: Essays in Honour of the Visionary Aboriginal Elder, David Burrumarra*. Indianapolis: Dog Ear Publishing.

Media, Miyarrka. 2011. *Manapanmirr, in Christmas Spirit*. Directed by Paul Gurrumuruwuy, Fiona Yangathu, Jennifer Deger and David Mackenzie. Gapuwiyak: Miyarrka Media.

Media, Miyarrka. 2014. *Ringtone*. Directed by Paul Gurrumuruwuy and Jennifer Deger. Australia: Ronin Films.

Media, Miyarrka. 2014a. *Christmas Birrimbirr*. Moesgaard Museum, Denmark.

Media, Miyarrka. 2014b. *Gapuwiyak Calling: Phone-Made Media from Arnhem Land*, edited by Jennifer Deger. St Lucia: University of Queensland, Anthropology Museum.

Michaels, Eric. 1993. *Bad Aboriginal Art: Tradition, Media, and Technological Horizons*. Minneapolis, MN: University of Minnesota Press.

Morphy, Frances. 2007. 'Performing Law: The Yolngu of Blue Mud Bay Meet the Native Title Process'. In *The Social Effects of Native Title: Recognition, Translation, Coexistence*, edited by Benjamin Smith and Frances Morphy, 31–57. Canberra: ANU ePress.

Morphy, Frances. 2008. 'Whose Governance, For Whose Good? The Laynhapuy Homelands Association and the Neo-Assimilationist Turn in Indigenous Policy'. In *Contested Governance: Culture, Power and Institutions in Indigenous Australia*, edited by Janet Hunt, Diane Smith, Stephanie Garling and Will Sanders. Canberra: ANU Press.

Morphy, Howard. 1989. 'From Dull to Brilliant: The Aesthetics of Spiritual Power Among the Yolngu'. *Man* 24 (1):21–40.

Morphy, Howard. 1991. *Ancestral Connections: Art and An Aboriginal System of Knowledge*. Chicago, IL: Chicago University Press.

Morphy, Howard. 2003. 'Cross-Cultural Categories, Yolngu Science and Local Discourses' (unpublished paper). Centre for Cross-Cultural Research, The Australian National University. http://livingknowledge.anu.edu.au/html/background/discussions/morphy_yolnguscience.htm.

Morphy, Howard. 2007. *Becoming Art: Exploring Cross-Cultural Categories*. Oxford and New York: Berg.

Morphy, Howard. 2013. 'The Art of Yirrkala Crayon Drawings: Innovation, Creativity and Tradition'. In *Yirrkala Crayon Drawings*, edited by Cara Pinchbeck. Sydney: The Art Gallery of New South Wales.

Morphy, Howard. 2015. 'Open Access vs The Culture of Protocols'. In *Museum as Process*, edited by Raymond A. Silverman, 90–104. Oxon and New York: Routledge.

Morphy, Howard, and Frances Morphy. 2006. 'Tasting the Waters: Discriminating Identities in the Waters of Blue Mud Bay'. *Journal of Material Culture* 11 (1/2):67–85.

Murray, Tom, and Allan Collins. 2004. *Dhakiyarr vs the King*. Alice Springs: CAAMA Productions.

Myers, Fred R. 2014. 'Showing Too Much or Too Little: Predicaments of Painting Indigenous Presence in Central Australia'. In *Performing Indigeneity: Global Histories and Contemporary Experiences*, edited by Laura R. Graham and H. Glenn Penny, 351–389. Nebraska: University of Nebraska Press.

Narayan, Kirin. 2016. *Everyday Creativity: Singing Godesses in the Himalayan Foothills*. Chicago, IL and London: Chicago University Press.

Navas, Eduardo, Owen Gallagher and xtine burrough, eds. 2015. *The Routledgge Companion to Remix Studies*. New York and Oxon: Routledge.

Neale, Timothy, Rodney Carter, Trent Nelson and Mick Bourke. 2019. 'Walking Together: A Decolonising Experiment in Bushfire Management on Dja Dja Wurrung Country'. *Cultural Geographies*: 1–19. https://journalssagepubcom.elibrary.jcu.edu.au/doi/10.1177/1474474018821419.

Pinchbeck, Cara, ed. 2018. *Noŋgirrŋa Marawili: From My Heart and Mind*. Sydney: Art Gallery of New South Wales.

Povinelli, Elizabeth. 2016. *Geontologies: A Requiem to Late Liberalism*. Durham, NC: Duke University Press.

Rennie, Ellie. 2013. 'Co-Creative Media in Remote Indigenous Communities'. *Cultural Science* 6 (1):23–36.

Roch, Jean and Steven Feld. 2003. *Cine-Ethnography*. Minneapolis, MN: University of Minnesota Press.

Schneider, A., and C. Wright. 2013. *Anthropology and Art Practice*. London: Bloomsbury.

Simpson, Audra. 2007. 'Ethnographic Refusal'. *Junctures* 9:67–80.

Skoggard, Ian, and Alisse Waterston. 2015. 'Introduction: Toward an Anthropology of Affect and Evocative Ethnography'. *Anthropology of Consciousness* 26 (2):109–120.

Smith, Linda Tuhiwai. 2012. *Decolonising Methodologies: Researching and Indigenous Peoples*, 2nd edn. Dunedin: Otago University Press.

Solnit, Rebecca. 2005. *A Fieldguide to Getting Lost*. London: Penguin.

Stewart, Kathleen. 2007. *Ordinary Affects*. Durham, NC: Duke University Press.

Sutton, Peter. 2011. *The Politics of Suffering*. Melbourne: Melbourne University Press.

Tamisari, Franca. 1998. 'Body, Vision and Movement: In the Footprints of the Ancestors'. *Oceania* 68 (4):249–270.

Tamisari, Franca. 2005. 'Writing Close to Dance: Expression in Yolngu Performance'. In *Aesthetics and Experience in Music Performance*, edited by E. Mackinlay, D. Collins and S. Owens, 165–190. Newcastle: Cambridge Scholars.

Tamisari, Franca. 2016. 'A Space and Time for a Generation to React: The Gattjirrk Cultural Festival in Milingimbi'. *Oceania* 86 (1):92–109.

Taussig, Michael. 2015. *The Corn Wolf*. Chicago, IL: University of Chicago Press.

Taussig, Michael. 2016 [1998]. 'Viscerality, faith, and skepticism: Another theory of magic'. HAU Journal of Ethnographic Theory 6(3):453–483.

Taylor, Mark C. 2014. *Recovering Place: Reflections on Stone Hill*. New York and Chichester: Columbia University Press.

Telban, Borut, and Daniela Vávrová. 2014. 'Ringing the Living and the Dead: Mobile Phones in a Sepik Society'. *The Australian Journal of Anthropology* 25 (2):223–238.

Thorner, Sabra, and John Dallwitz. 2015. 'Storytelling Photographs, Animating Anangu: How Ara Irititja – An Indigenous Digital Archive in Central Australia – Facilitates Cultural Reproduction'. In *Technology and Digital Initiatives: Innovative Approaches for Museums*, edited by Juilee Decker, 53–60. London: Rowman & Littlefield.

Toner, Peter G. 2001. 'When the Echoes Are Gone: A Yolngu Musical Anthropology'. PhD dissertation, Anthropology, Australian National University.

Toner, Peter G. 2003. 'Melody and the Musical Articulation of Yolngu Identities'. *Yearbook for Traditional Music* 35:69–95.

Tsing, Anna Lowenhaupt. 2015. *The Mushroom at the End of the World: On the Possibility of Life in Capitalist Ruins*. Princeton, NJ: Princeton University Press.

Turkle, Sherry 2011. *Alone Together: Why We Expect More from Technology and Less from Each Other*. New York: Basic Books.

Vaarzon-Morel, Petronella. 2014. 'Pointing the Phone: Transforming Technologies and Social Relations among Warlpiri'. *The Australian Journal of Anthropology* 25:239–255.

Verran, Helen, and Michael Christie. 2014. 'Postcolonial Databasing? Subverting Old Appropriations, Developing New Associations'. In *Subversion, Conversion, Development: Diversity and the Adoption and Use of Information and Communication Technologies*, edited by J. Leach and L. Wilson. Cambridge, MA: The MIT Press.

Verran, Helen, and Michael Christie. 2014. 'Digital Lives in Postcolonial Australia'. *Journal of Material Culture* 18(3):299-317.

Verran, Helen, Michael Christie, Bryce Anbins-King, Trevor van Weeren and Wulumdhuna Yunupingu. 2007. 'Designing Digital Knowledge Management Tools with Aboriginal Australians'. *Digital Creativity* 18 (3):129–142.

Vokes, Richard. 2016. 'Before the Call: Mobile Phones, Exchange Relations, and Social Change in South-Western Uganda'. *Ethnos* 10.1080/00141844.2015.1133689.

Vokes, Richard and Katrien Pype. 2018. 'Chronotopes of Media in Sub-Saharan Africa'. *Ethnos* 83(2):207–217.

von Sturmer, John. 2008. 'A Limping World: Works in the Arnott's Collection – Some Conceptual Underpinnings. In *They are Meditating: Bark Paintings from the MCA's Arnott's Collection*, 35–53. Sydney: Museum of Contemporary Art.

Warner, W. Lloyd. 1969 [1937]. *A Black Civilization: A Social Study of an Australian Tribe*. Gloucester, MA: Peter Smith.

Williams, Nancy. 1986. *The Yolngu and Their Land: A System of Land Tenure and the Fight for Its Recognition*. Canberra: Australian Institute of Aboriginal Studies.

Young, Diana. 2006. 'The Colours of Things'. In *The Handbook of Material Culture*, edited by P. Spyer, C. Tilley, S. Kuechler and W. Keane, 173–185. London, Thousand Oaks, CA and New Delhi: Sage.

Young, Diana. 2011. 'Mutable Things: Colours as Material Practice in the North West of South Australia'. *Journal of the Royal Anthropological Institute* 17 (2):356–376.

Young, Diana, ed. 2018. *Rematerializing Colour: From Concept to Substance*. Canon Pyon: Sean Kingston Publishing.

Zorc, R. David. 1995. *Yolŋu Matha Dictionary*. Batchelor, NT: School of Australian Linguistics, Darwin Institute of Technology.

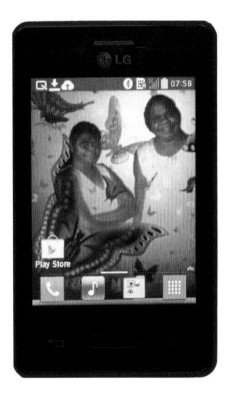

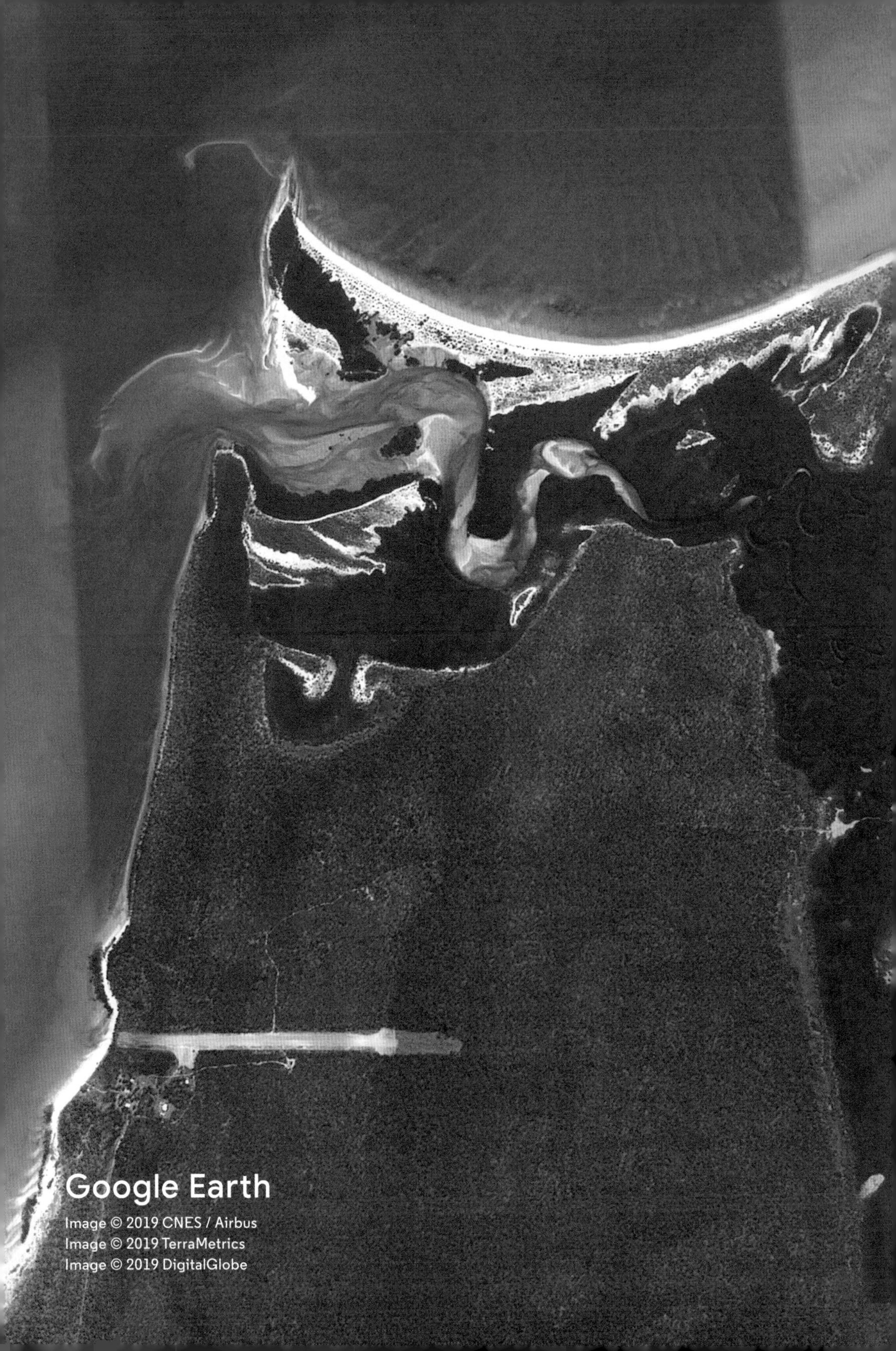

Google Earth
Image © 2019 CNES / Airbus
Image © 2019 TerraMetrics
Image © 2019 DigitalGlobe

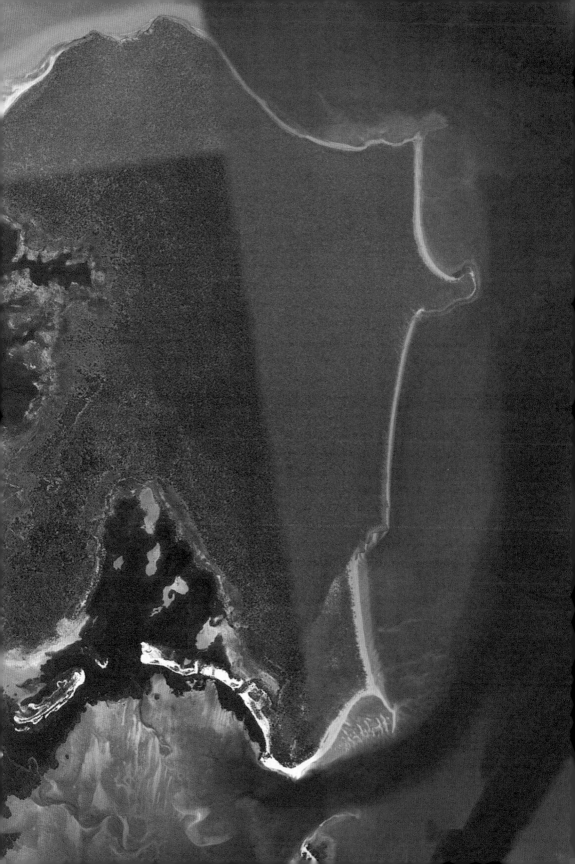

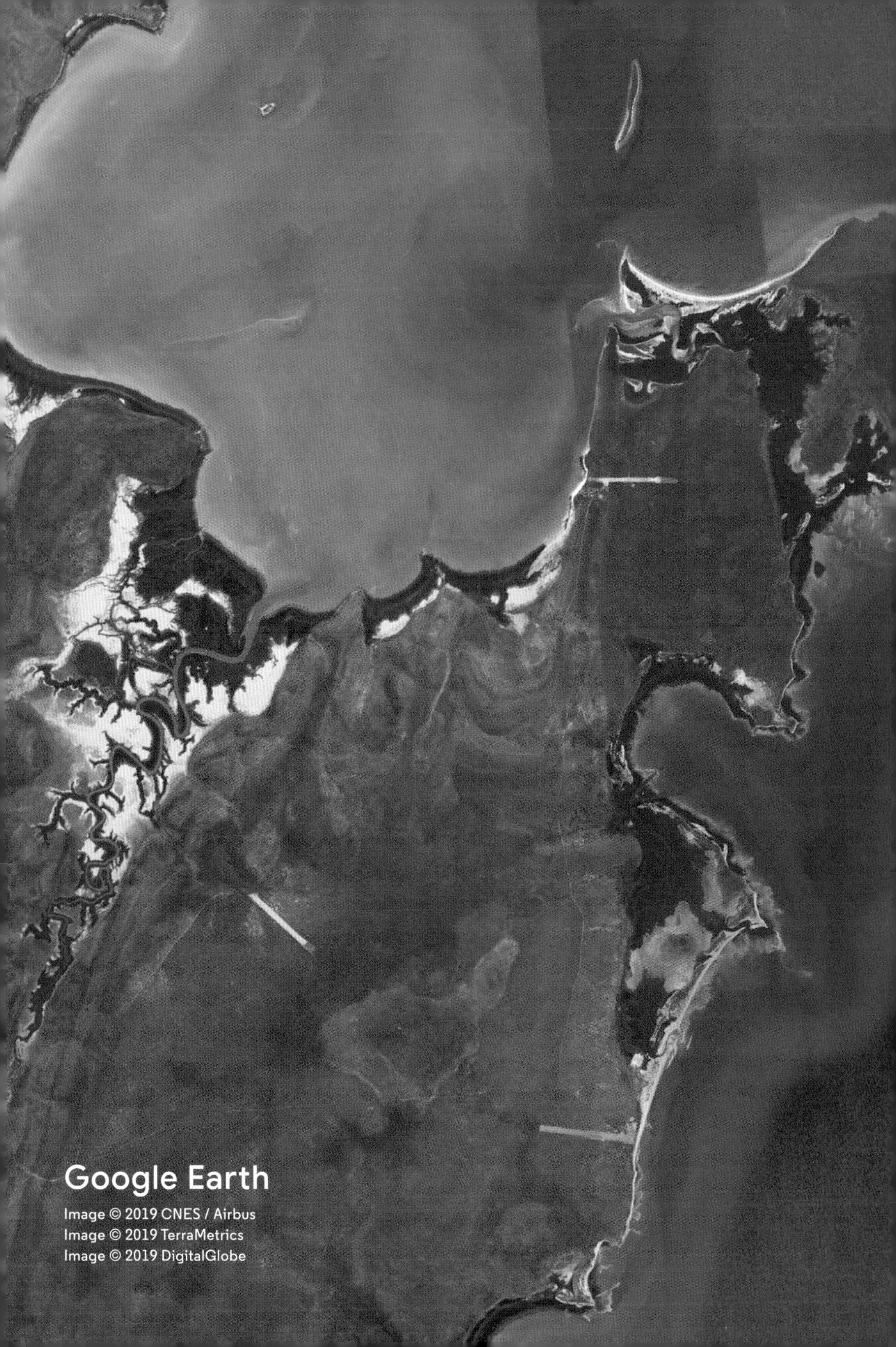
Google Earth
Image © 2019 CNES / Airbus
Image © 2019 TerraMetrics
Image © 2019 DigitalGlobe

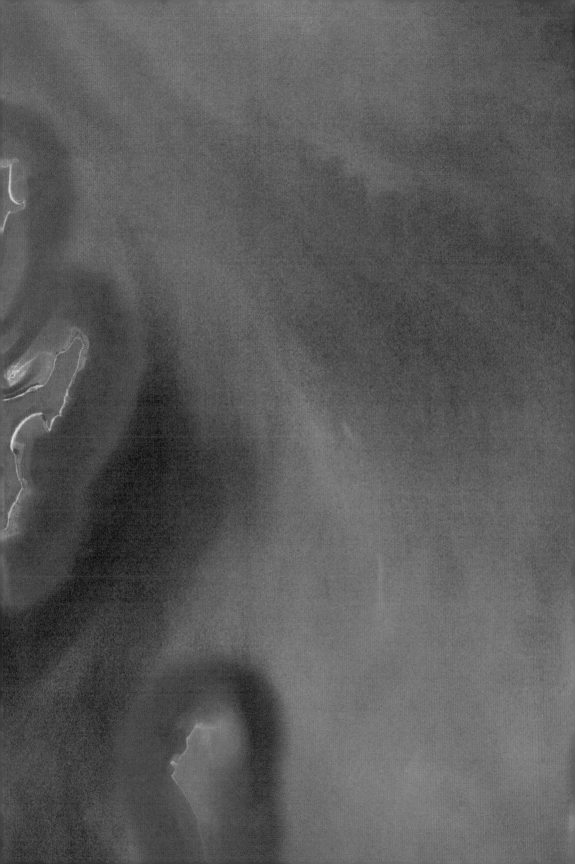

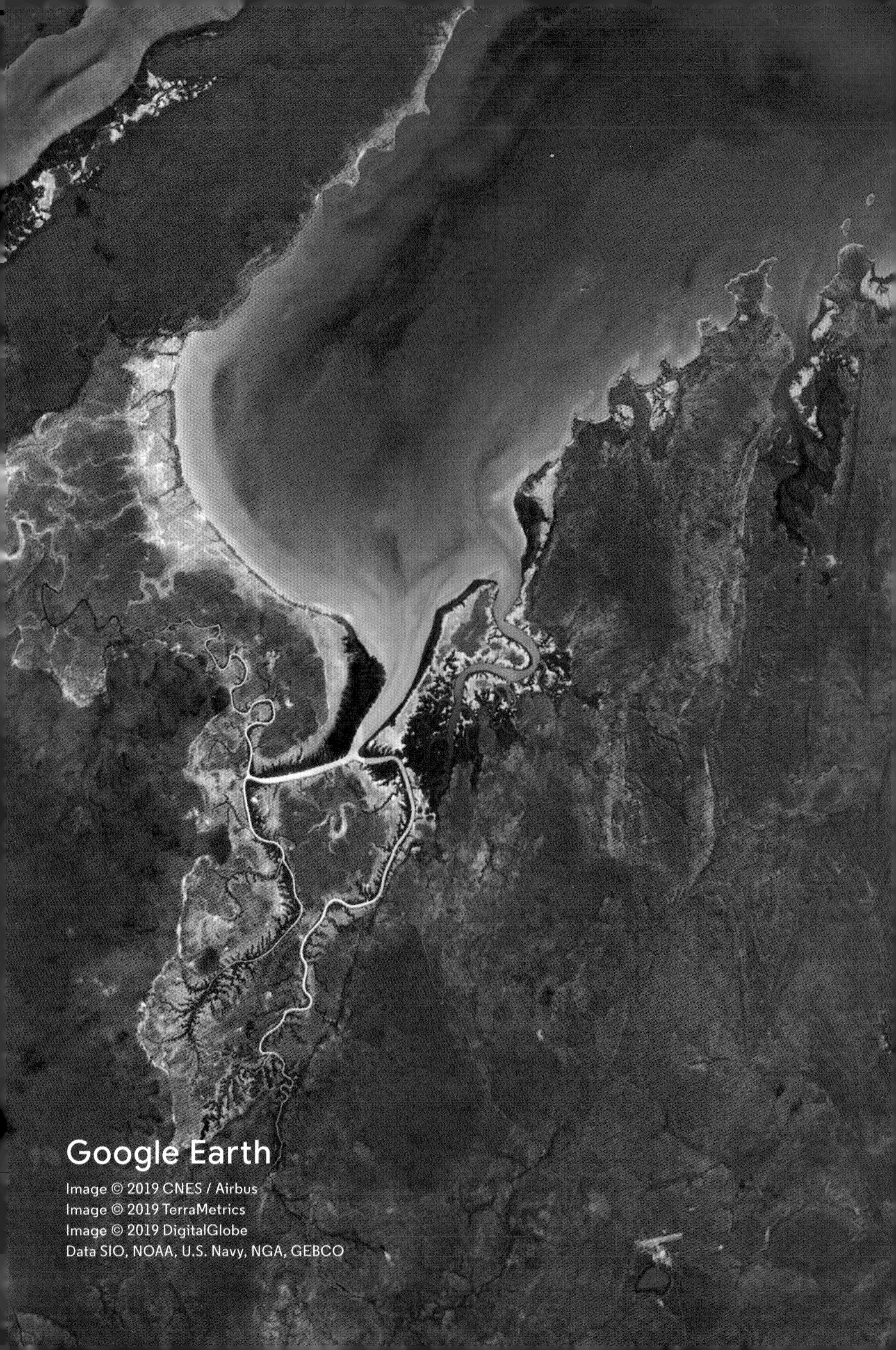
Google Earth
Image © 2019 CNES / Airbus
Image © 2019 TerraMetrics
Image © 2019 DigitalGlobe
Data SIO, NOAA, U.S. Navy, NGA, GEBCO